SMALL BUSINESS MANAGEMENT SERIES

....

Marketing for a Small Business

....

Other books in the Small Business Management Series:

Entrepreneurship and How to Establish Your Own Business

Basic Principles of Financial Management for a Small Business

For publication by the end of 1996:

Management of a Small Business

Important Information for a Successful Business

Growth and the Different Phases of a Business

How to Franchise Your Own Business

Alternative Methods of Obtaining a Business: Buy an Existing Business,
Franchise or Home Industry

Import, Export and Internationalisation of a Business

Strategic Management of a Small Business

Entrepreneurship and Entrepreneurial Skills

Series Co-ordinating Editor:
Cecile Nieuwenhuizen

About the author ...

Ricardo Machado is a senior lecturer in the Department of Business Economics at the University of South Africa. He holds the degrees BSc and MBA, and he holds an Honours degree in Marketing. He has co-authored other books on Marketing.

SMALL BUSINESS MANAGEMENT SERIES

....

Marketing for a Small Business

....

by

Ricardo Machado

First published 1996

ISBN 0 7021 3554 2

© Juta & Co. Ltd.
P.O. Box 14373, Kenwyn 7790

Editing: Jacquie Withers

Didactic Adviser: Anna-Marie Bates, Centre for Courseware Design and Development, Technikon SA

Book design and typesetting: Charlene Bate, Cape Town

Illustrations: Mark Bates

Icons: Carol Nelson

Cover design: Inspiration Sandwich

Printed in South Africa by Creda Press, Eliot Avenue, Eppindust II

This book is dedicated to my parents

PREFACE

The growing importance of small business in South Africa has led to the development of many books applying the theories of business management to the small business sector. This book applies the basic principles of marketing to the small business scenario. The book begins with an overview of marketing and then takes the reader through a step by step process designed to help him/her both understand and work through the contents. The reader also has a brief case study and a self evaluation section for each chapter to help integrate the contents.

The text has been written in a concise and reader friendly manner, so that the reader will be able to become easily conversant with all aspects of small business marketing. Concepts are clearly explained and the process of developing a marketing plan is summarised. This book will help answer the questions of many small business persons as to how to market their products or business.

This exciting text is ideally suited for use by those wanting a basic grounding in marketing for a small business and for business owners who are looking for an easy to follow guide for developing a market plan.

R Machado
December 1995

KEY TO ICONS

Four icons are used throughout this text to depict different components of the interactive learning process:

Example

Definition

Note well

Activity

CONTENTS

CHAPTER 3: CHOOSING TO WHOM TO MARKET: PINPOINTING THE TARGET MARKET

CHAPTER 4:   PRODUCT DECISIONS: WHAT EXACTLY DO WE OFFER OUR CUSTOMERS?

CHAPTER 5: PRICE: HOW TO DETERMINE WHAT TO CHARGE?

CHAPTER 6: DISTRIBUTION: GETTING YOUR PRODUCT TO THE CUSTOMER

CHAPTER 7: PROMOTION: COMMUNICATING WITH YOUR MARKET

CHAPTER 8: THE MARKETING PLAN: PUTTING IT ALL TOGETHER

1 ORIENTATION TO MARKETING

1 LEARNING OBJECTIVES

After you have studied this chapter you should be able to:

❑ define what is meant by marketing
❑ explain the role of marketing in satisfying customer needs
❑ summarise marketing strategies with respect to:
  – the role of product as an instrument in marketing
  – the role of price as an instrument in marketing
  – the role of promotion as an instrument in marketing
  – the role of distribution as an instrument in marketing.

2 INTRODUCTION

Good marketing is probably one of the most important areas on which to focus if you want to ensure that your small business succeeds. This is because marketing deals with two aspects which are critical to any business – its **customers** and its **competitors**. Marketing is what enables your business to be competitive and successful out in the market place (as it is called). It is important then that every business owner have a marketing orientation.

Having a marketing orientation means that you must establish:
❑ **customer satisfaction; and**
❑ **maximum profit**
as the two most important long-term goals of your business. All other business functions and activities which you perform in your business must be done with these two goals in mind. The marketing orientation must be the driving force in your business.

3 MARKETING: THE LINK BETWEEN BUSINESS AND CUSTOMERS

Marketing has been defined as the performance of business activities that **direct the flow of goods and services from producer to consumer (i.e. customer or user).** What does this mean? It means that marketing includes all the activities done by you for customers to be able to have the right goods or services at the right price at a convenient place or time. This definition of marketing highlights the fact that for a business to be really effective, it must ensure that **meeting customer needs** is a philosophy in which all in the

1

business not only believe but actually make happen in the course of their work. You can see that marketing affects the entire business.

Although this is a good general definition of marketing, it does not really tell a small business person exactly what marketing is. What you need is a definition of marketing which relates to small business!

A good definition of small business marketing is provided by Longenecker, Moore & Petty (1994:190).

Small business marketing consists of those business activities that relate directly to identifying target markets, determining the potential of the target market, and preparing, communicating and delivering some bundle of satisfaction to the target markets.

This means that marketing includes finding out who your customers (target market) will be, and making sure that everything that you do, or offer to those customers, is done in such a way that they are satisfied. A bundle of satisfaction would be made up of your **product, your service, the way you promote your product, the prices of the product and your after-sales follow up.**

Small business marketing entails identifying target markets, determining their potential, and preparing, communicating and delivering satisfaction to these target markets.

This definition helps to highlight the marketing activities which are important for every small business. Figure 1 shows how these marketing activities relate to the four key decision areas in marketing. When you combine these **key decision areas** (product, price, promotion and distribution) with the aim of satisfying a specific target market, we term the combination *'the marketing mix'*.

FIGURE 1
SMALL BUSINESS MARKETING ACTIVITIES

DEFINITION OF SMALL BUSINESS MARKETING	MARKETING ACTIVITY	AREAS OF IMPORTANCE
❑ Identifying target markets		
❑ Determining target market potential	Market research Segmenting a market Sales forecasting	Analysing the market ☞

DEFINITION OF SMALL BUSINESS MARKETING	MARKETING ACTIVITY	AREAS OF IMPORTANCE
❏ Preparing a bundle of satisfaction	Product Pricing Promotion	
❏ Communicating a bundle of satisfaction	Communication	Marketing mix
❏ Delivering a bundle of satisfaction	Distribution	

Source: Adapted from Longenecker, J.G. Moore, C.W., Petty, J.W. 1994. *Small business management: an entrepreneurial emphasis.* 9th edition. South Western: Cincinnati, p. 190.

Small business owners or entrepreneurs often get involved in aspects of business that distract their attention from the effort to satisfy customers. This is a sure route to ruin! A small business person cannot satisfy every customer's needs. Further, you will usually not be the cheapest producer or supplier.

As a small business person, though, you will have some **advantages** and you must make the most of these. Small businesses are usually better acquainted with customers than large, bureaucratic businesses. Because of your size, you can respond quickly to change, and you can follow a hands-on approach in your management of the business.

Other advantages of being a small company include the ability to profit from small groups of customers in the market (groups that may be too small for your competitor), and the potential for all your staff to interact with customers.

The role of marketing for your business should be to make your business and what it offers transparent to the customers to whom you have chosen to offer your product/service, and their needs or requirements transparent to your business.

Marketing is the link between your business and customers.

You give customers something of value (product/service) and they give you something of value (usually money, goods or services). Always keep that in mind – being in business is a two-way exchange between you and your customers. Marketing is the *link* between your business and your customers.

1. Name two advantages of a small business as opposed to a large, bureaucratic business.

   ....

2. Explain in your own words:
   "Marketing is the link between your business and your customer"

   ....

4 WHY IS THE LINK NECESSARY?

The link is necessary because there are gaps or differences between a business (producer/manufacturer) and its customer which must be overcome.

	FIGURE 2 **GAPS BETWEEN THE BUSINESS AND ITS CUSTOMERS**
spatial gap	the geographic separation between a business and its customers *(you have only one location for your store)*
time gap	customers do not want goods at the time they are produced *(you only make buns on a Sunday)*
information gap	producers don't know what customers want – customers do not know what is available from producers nor at what terms *(your customers do not know when your sale begins)* SALE SOON
value gap	producers value goods in terms of costs and competitive prices – customers value goods in terms of what they can do for them *(customers can't see why, in their opinion, you are so expensive)*
ownership gap	producers have title to or own goods that they do not want to consume *(customers want to consume goods that they do not own)*

| quantity discrepancy or gap | producers prefer to sell in large quantities – customers prefer to buy in small quantities *(your customers want only one metre of material; you sell in five metre lots)* |  |
| assortment discrepancy or gap | producers specialise in producing a narrow assortment of goods and services – consumers need a broad assortment from which to choose *(you only stock one kind of cigarette)* |  |

Source: Adapted from McCarthy, E.J. & Perrault, W.D. 1990. *Basic marketing*. Irwin: Homewood, p. 18.

Remember that marketing is the link between your business and your customers. Through the marketing-related activities that you will follow, your business will overcome these gaps and differences. These marketing-related activities include finding and choosing customers, selling, promoting, transporting, storing, financing and the like.

Finding out who your customers will be

The most important decision that a small business marketer can make is to **identify the target market** for the business. Scarborough & Zimmerer (1988:485) provide a good definition of a target market.

> **A target market is the specific group of customers at whom the business aims its goods or services.**

The better you understand and define your targeted customer, the better chance you will have of success. Once identified, this target customer (or target market) will influence *all* aspects of the business. This includes the product (or merchandise), the way your business looks, the pricing – everything. Without knowing the target market a small business often tries to reach everyone and often ends up appealing to no-one!

Suppose we were going to open a shoe repair outlet in central Johannesburg. The target market would most probably be office workers who come into town to work and who need quick, economical repairs!

Therefore, the question to ask yourself is: **Do you know your customers well enough to be able to choose a target market confidently?**

It is not good enough simply to give a quick or unconsidered answer to this question – it requires careful answers based on analysis. If you do not know who your customers are, you cannot know what their needs are.

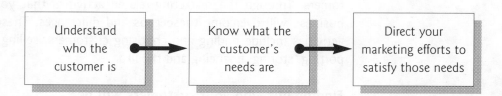

| Understand who the customer is | → | Know what the customer's needs are | → | Direct your marketing efforts to satisfy those needs |

You should be trying to identify the groups of people most likely to buy and the common characteristics among them. The idea is to be able to build a **customer profile** of the people who have a common need, and then try to satisfy that need. This will give you the ability to discover the crucial group of customers for your business, and doing this will ensure the success of your business.

QUESTIONS YOU SHOULD BE ABLE TO ANSWER ABOUT YOUR MARKET

- ❑ What is your target market?
- ❑ What is the size of your target market?
- ❑ What is the profile of your target customer?
- ❑ Are there any specific major customers and, if so, who are they?
- ❑ How will customers benefit by using your product or service?
- ❑ How loyal are they to their present suppliers?
- ❑ How much of the potential market do you expect to get?
- ❑ What factors cause them to increase or decrease their buying?
- ❑ What are the trends in the market?

Source: Adapted from Longenecker, J.G., Moore, C.W. & Petty, J.W. 1994. *Small business management: an entrepreneurial emphasis*. South Western: Cincinnati, p. 179.

In order to build a customer profile you will need to be able to answer a number of pertinent questions about your customer. The table below shows typical questions used in building a customer profile, in this case for a shoe repair store in central Johannesburg.

TYPICAL QUESTIONS TO BE ANSWERED IN COMPILING A CUSTOMER PROFILE	
Customer Profile Questions	**Answers**
education level?	all levels, mostly matric
geographic area?	central Johannesburg only
rural, suburban, urban?	urban customers only
ethnic group?	all races
individuals, other businesses?	concentrate on the individual
men, women, children, families?	many women, but mostly men
age group?	16-65 years old
income group?	middle income group
lifestyles?	typical city worker, has not got much time, wants quick service
buying patterns?	uses shoe repair services while going to and from work, lunchtimes
usage patterns?	heavy users of shoes, tend to walk a lot

Note that the questions in the profile above are not final: you may add or leave out questions as you see fit. The idea is to have the right questions and enough of them to be able to describe your customer really well. The most successful businesses have very well defined descriptions of the customers that they are trying to attract.

A customer profile is a description of your potential customers.

Note that if you have several target markets each target group should have its *own* target profile.

What could the result be of an incomplete customer profile?

. . . .

. . . .

5 COMPETITIVE EDGE

It is often surprising how little most small business people know about their competition. Indeed, it often seems as if the business person thinks that he/she is the only one offering customers that specific product or service! The business person must **identify competitors** and study them carefully. They must be analysed in terms of **what they offer**, as well as **how they are managed** and what their **strengths and weaknesses** are. In fact, this analysis of the competition is often required when applying for a loan or finance to begin a business and if it is missing the knowledge of the entrepreneur in respect of his/her business could be questioned!

QUESTIONS YOU SHOULD BE ABLE TO ANSWER ABOUT YOUR COMPETITORS

❑ Who are your strongest competitors?
❑ Are their businesses growing or not?
❑ How does your business compare with that of your competitors?
❑ In what areas do you have advantages over your competitors?
❑ In what areas are you weaker than your competitors?
❑ What is your competitive edge?

Source: Adapted from Longenecker, J.G., Moore, C.W. & Petty, J.W. 1994. *Small business management: an entrepreneurial emphasis.* South Western: Cincinnati, p. 179.

Why should you do this analysis of the competition? One of the main benefits of analysing your competition is that it helps you, as a small business person, to develop a competitive edge. Scarborough & Zimmerer (1988:486) state that a company has a competitive edge when customers can see that its products or services are superior to those of its competitors. Your job is to create this competitive edge in the minds of your customers.

A competitive edge is what you have when customers can see that your products or services are superior to those of your competitors.

Business people often try to get a competitive edge by offering lower prices. This is dangerous, because it is often not a lasting advantage and, further, it is easily copied – the competition can simply match it. The fact that you are a small business gives you the opportunity to develop other competitive edges, for example:
❑ a close contact with customers
❑ personal attention
❑ good service
❑ flexibility

In our example of the shoe repair outlet in central Johannesburg, we might establish our competitive edge by picking up and delivering shoes for repair free of charge so that customers would not have to come to us.

Below is a list of some possible competitive edges which you might use. If you decide to use service as your competitive edge then look at the indicators of good service shown below to see if these apply to you.

POSSIBLE COMPETITIVE EDGES YOU MIGHT USE	EXAMPLE
❑ being close to your customers	visit customers every week
❑ giving customers personal attention	having enough salespeople to help customers quickly
❑ providing excellent service	delivering and invoicing within one hour
❑ being flexible and able to respond quickly	developing a new product for a customer within a week or two
❑ providing consistently high quality	checking your products personally before delivery
❑ being innovative in the market place	creating new products before the competitors do
❑ having a good location	being located in an area that is easy to reach

You have opened a shoe repair outlet in central Johannesburg. You decide to look at your biggest competitor who is two blocks away. You find out that they have been at that location for 15 years. Your customers tell you that they have a very good reputation but that they have become very expensive lately. You also notice that the owner of the shop is very rude to customers and that he refuses to give you your money back if the repairs are not to your satisfaction; he simply fixes it again. Your bank manager told you that the owner has done very well for himself at that shop and is financially very sound.

Identify the competitor's :

Strengths   Weaknesses

1 ....   1 ....

2 ....   2 ....

3 ....   3 ....

4 ....   4 ....

If you choose good service as your competitive edge you must make sure that your customers get that good service and that they can see it and are aware of it. Below is a group of indicators of good service – see if they apply to your business!

INDICATORS OF GOOD SERVICE

- ❑ waiting customers are acknowledged
- ❑ all transactions are handled quickly and efficiently
- ❑ staff have a sound knowledge of location of goods
- ❑ staff knowledge of stock situation re sizes, colours, etc. is sound
- ❑ staff have a good knowledge of product features and usage
- ❑ communication with customers is friendly
- ❑ promises to customers are kept
- ❑ alternative sales possibilities are discussed

Once you understand the customer and have determined what your competitive edge is you can decide on your **marketing strategy.**

⑥ MARKETING STRATEGY

The marketing strategy is one of the most important areas to those who may **invest** in or **provide finance** to a small business. The marketing strategy will guide the business as to how to satisfy its customers. Once the target group of customers has been identified, the small business person has to develop the **mix of marketing tools** (product, price, promotion, distribution) which will best satisfy the target market's needs. This is called the marketing mix (see Figure 3).

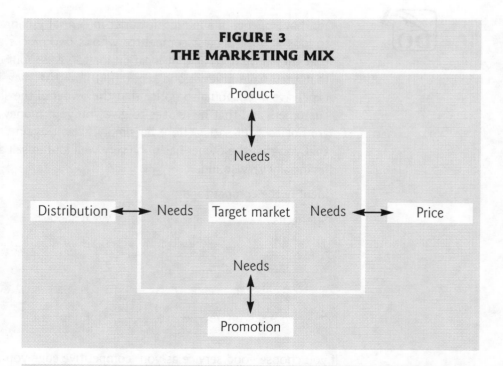

FIGURE 3
THE MARKETING MIX

The marketing mix is the mix of product, price, promotion and distribution that best satisfies the needs of the target market.

A common way of explaining it is that the marketing mix is how the small business person gets the **right product** to the **right place** at the **right time** at the **right price** and **lets the customer know** about it!

The type of business you have, as well as whether or not it is a new business, will have an effect on how much emphasis is given to each of the areas of the marketing mix. Let's briefly summarise each of the four areas, and illustrate them with the example of *HDL Jewellery* located in Bloemfontein (Van der Walt & Machado, 1992:213-217). Each of the four areas of the marketing mix will also be explained in more detail later in the book.

6.1 Product/Service

In this area you need to decide exactly what you are going to offer the customers that you have chosen. Here you will have to identify the **major product/service types** that you will offer as well as the **associated or supporting products/services.** You will also have to decide on a **name** for your business and/or product. Another component of the product is the **packaging.** This is important as customers see both the name and the packaging as part of the product. The supporting products/services mentioned above relate directly to the need satisfaction of your chosen target market.

The products offered by HDL include fine jewellery, designer jewellery, costume jewellery, silver jewellery, pearls, expensive watches and trophies. The supporting services at HDL include the design, manufacturing, wholesaling and retailing of fine jewellery.

We can see that HDL has a wide range of products (i.e. the product mix) and supporting services in an effort to meet its customers' needs.

ASPECTS OF THE PRODUCT/SERVICE:

- ❑ actual product/service
- ❑ supporting product/service
- ❑ product mix
- ❑ product name or brand
- ❑ packaging
- ❑ supporting services

6.2 Pricing

In this area of the marketing mix you determine **what the customer will pay** for the need satisfaction that you offer. You will have to have a good **knowledge of all your costs,** such as production and marketing. You will also need to know what the competitor's prices are, and what sort of flexibility you will need in terms of discounts, allowances and deals.

HDL's target market is the middle and higher income groups, so it aims at being competitively priced when compared with other suppliers of jewellery aiming at this target market. Since a great deal of its work is in designing jewellery for customers, HDL is able to establish fair but reasonable profit margins.

Pricing, therefore, directly affects the profitability of your business and is dependant on the target market that you choose.

ASPECTS OF PRICING:	
❏ cost	❏ marketing costs
❏ competitive prices	❏ production costs
❏ selling price	❏ fixed costs
❏ discounts	❏ variable costs
❏ allowances	❏ expected price

6.3 Promotion

This area of the marketing mix deals with how you are going to **make your target market aware** of what you offer as well as why they should buy your product/service. There are many ways of doing this, for example advertising, sales promotion, personal selling, publicity, direct promotion, outdoor posters and so on. The choices are endless and often innovation is needed. The **competitive edge** that we mentioned will have to be communicated, and the **design of the advertising** and **choice of message** are important. Many small business people do their own promotion or use the services of other small businesses who offer this service as *their* product!

HDL Jewellery uses publicity, receptions and parties, personal selling and exhibitions to promote its products. It obtains publicity through hosting receptions for groups of customers such as women's organisations and housewives.

It also gives talks on request and the owner is often invited to speak at events. Personal selling is used at the store and HDL makes sure all its sales staff are well trained in terms of both product knowledge and selling techniques. HDL also regularly exhibits product(s) at shows, such as agricultural shows. When this is planned letters are sent to as many people as possible in the small town where the show is being held, inviting them to attend.

Promotion is important because it is the way to inform and communicate with your customers. Through promotion you can persuade them as to the benefits for them of buying your product.

ASPECTS OF PROMOTION:	
❑ choice of media	❑ design of advertising
❑ choice of message	❑ choice of agency
❑ budget	❑ direct mail database
❑ advertising	❑ prospecting system for identifying
❑ sales promotion	customers
❑ publicity	❑ personal selling

6.4 Distribution

This area of the marketing mix is where you decide **how you are going to get your product to the target market.**

You may go **direct** to customers or you may **use other people** to reach those customers for you. This may mean having to convince other people to stock your product. If your business needs a **location,** it will also be dealt with here, and in the process you will have to decide how it will be set up. Further, your business may have **export opportunities,** and this will also be dealt with as an aspect of distribution.

HDL distributes its products to customers through its store in Bloemfontein and also through agents working for commission on a regional basis.

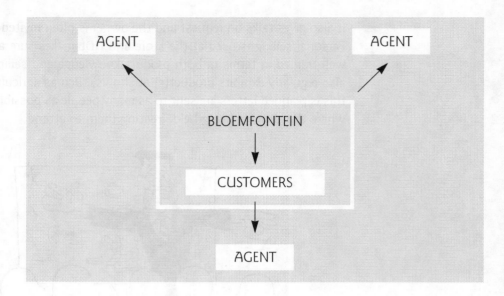

Distribution can thus be seen as how your business gets its product to the target market. Keep in mind that your aim here is to make it easy for your customers to purchase your products.

ASPECTS OF DISTRIBUTION:

- ❏ channel to the customer
- ❏ location of store
- ❏ store layout
- ❏ export coverage

7 SELF-EVALUATION

7.1 Terms you have learned

EXPLAIN EACH OF THE FOLLOWING:

- ❏ marketing
- ❏ small business marketing
- ❏ marketing mix
- ❏ target market
- ❏ customer profile
- ❏ competitive edge

7.2 QUIZ

Answer the following questions.

Fill in the missing words:

(a) (i) Basing your business on satisfying customer needs is one aspect of the .... orientation.

14

(ii) Market research, segmenting a market and sales forecasting are examples of .... activities.

(iii) Marketing is the .... between your business and your customer.

(b) What are the advantages of a small business in terms of marketing. (Name at least 3 advantages.)

....

....

....

(c) List seven possible gaps between a business and its customers.

....

....

....

....

(d) What is a customer profile?

....

....

....

(e) List five possible areas in which you can gain a competitive edge.

1 ....

2 ....

3 ....

4 ....

5 ....

(f) What is a marketing mix?

....

....

....

(g) What are the four major aspects of a marketing mix?

1 ....

2 ....

3 ....

4 ....

(h)   What could be the competitive edge for a computer training company?

....

....

....

7.3 Case Study

HDL JEWELLERY

HDL Jewellery began as a hobby out of a farmhouse, and grew into a large, successful business. Dolores Loubser, the owner of HDL, won Old Mutual's Small Businesswoman of 1986' award. Dolores first went to a large jewellery show to ask jewellery customers and suppliers questions in order to find out about customer needs. She even wrote over a thousand letters to jewellers and manufacturers all over the world to get information about jewellery and customers. From this, she decided to focus on designing and making exclusive jewellery for middle to high income groups. She relies on parties and receptions, personal selling and exhibitions/demonstrations to provide publicity for her product. She ascribes her success to the personal contact she keeps with the community she serves.

Source: Van der Walt, A. & Machado, R. (eds.). 1992. *New marketing success stories*. Southern: Johannesburg, pp. 213-217.

Name four reasons for the success of Dolores Loubser of HDL, as shown by her winning the Small Businesswoman of the Year award.

....

....

8 REFERENCES

Longenecker, J.G., Moore, C.W. & Petty, J.W. 1994. *Small business management: an entrepreneurial emphasis*. 9th edition. South Western: Cincinnati.

McCarthy, E.J. & Perrault, W.D. 1990. *Basic marketing*. Irwin: Homewood.

Scarborough, N.M. & Zimmerer, T.W. 1988. *Effective small business management*. 2nd edition. Merill: Columbus.

Van der Walt, A. & Machado, R. (eds.). 1992. *New marketing success stories*. Southern.: Johannesburg.

GETTING AND USING MARKETING INFORMATION

2

1 LEARNING OBJECTIVES

After you have studied this chapter you should be able to:

- ❏ explain why you need marketing information
- ❏ explain what marketing research is
- ❏ state the advantages of using marketing research
- ❏ describe the process involved in doing marketing research
- ❏ define secondary information and the various types of secondary information
- ❏ define primary information
- ❏ list the five methods for getting primary information
- ❏ formulate the types of questions to use in a survey

2 INTRODUCTION

Many entrepreneurs and business people believe that "you must make things happen". This may lead the business person to make quick decisions based only on what he/she thinks or feels is right. This instinct or "gut feel" is always an important part of any marketing decision, but it is also necessary to have access to good marketing information. It may be a good idea to wait on the decision until you have some **facts** to help you. These facts, or information, cannot guarantee a correct decision – but having sound information is probably one of the more important contributors to being able to make really good and effective decisions.

Some common sources of information include **current customers,** contacts with **other business people**, and your **own instinct or "gut feel"** (Longenecker *et al*, 1994:192). The more information that a business has, the better it can understand its market, customers and competitors. The most common way of getting that information is through **marketing research.**

EXAMPLES OF SOURCES OF INFORMATION FOR NEW PRODUCTS

A survey done on small and medium businesses in the United States identified some of the sources of information used for developing new products/services. These were:

❑	current customers	73%
❑	contact with colleagues and other entrepreneurs	52%
❑	own instinct	46%
❑	informal poll of potential customers	43%
❑	information on companies in the industry	41%
❑	trade journals	35%
❑	focus groups	15%
❑	seminars and courses	14%
❑	consulting or research companies	8%
❑	public libraries	6%
❑	local universities	4%

Source: Adapted from Longenecker, J.G., Moore, C.W. & Petty, J.W. 1994. *Small business management: an entrepreneurial emphasis.* South Western: Cincinnati, p. 193.

3 WHAT IS MARKETING RESEARCH?

Marketing research is identifying what information you need, going out and getting that information, looking at the information to try to determine what it tells you about the customers, competitors or markets that you are in, and then doing something in your business based on that information.

Marketing research is the collecting, analysing and interpreting of marketing information pertaining to the customers, competitors or market.

(Scarborough & Zimmerer, 1988:482)

MARKETING RESEARCH

Crimp (1985:3) provides another useful definition.

Marketing research is the means used by those who provide goods and services to keep themselves in touch with the needs and wants of those who buy and use those goods and services.

According to Longenecker *et al* (1994:193), small business people often perform less marketing research than bigger businesses. This is due to:

❑ a lack of understanding as to how or what marketing research is
❑ the costs involved

These two factors can be overcome through using practical and economical methods. For example, your existing customers can be used for doing research, you can use students to do your actual research, and you can ask your customers a couple of question by telephone.

FOUR COMMON MISCONCEPTIONS ABOUT MARKETING RESEARCH

1. Marketing research means you do surveys.
2. It costs so much only big organisations can conduct marketing research.
3. It is complex and difficult so only "fundis" can do it.
4. Most of the time marketing research tells you things you already knew.

Marketing research should be used by all small business people. Why do we say this? In a small business, the financial situation is usually tight and money is scarce. A small business cannot afford to make mistakes, and marketing research will **reduce the risk of making a bad decision**. In fact, as we have said before, a small business person often has the advantage over bigger businesses in being closer to customers and to the market. Marketing research can help you **learn something new** about a market or **discover changes** taking place in your customers. It also helps you to stay up to date in terms of knowledge about your customers.

Given the many good things that marketing research can achieve, why do some business people never use it? Scarborough and Zimmerer (1988:483) identify some of the possible reasons. They are:

❑ not having enough time to do research
❑ not having enough knowledge about how to do research
❑ not having enough money to do research
❑ not being able to use the results practically

However, making decisions without using any marketing research could lead to problems.

THE RESULTS OF MAKING DECISIONS WITHOUT ANY RESEARCH

- ❑ poor locations
- ❑ improper product lines
- ❑ inappropriate prices
- ❑ bad choices leading to failure

Source: Scarborough, N.M. & Zimmerer, T.W. 1988. *Effective small business management*. 2nd edition. Merrill Publishing: Columbus, p. 483.

The point is, though, that marketing research does not have to be difficult or expensive to be useful. It also does not take up a lot of your time. It can be done informally, and just by trying to get information together you may get valuable insights into your business or customers, which can help you to produce better results.

SIMPLE RESEARCH CAN PRODUCE RESULTS

A construction company in San Francisco in the United States was trying to find itself a competitive edge. It decided to do some market research, and the way it went about it was to ask customers about its competitor's worst habits. The customers mentioned some of these, which included being impolite, uncaring about the dirt workers brought into a house, and staff and equipment that looked shoddy. This did not go down well with the majority of customers, who were fairly wealthy.

This information convinced the construction company to improve its image. It bought new equipment, kept it spotless, trained its workers to be polite, and dressed them well so as to give a good image.

The research and changes paid off. In less than two years, the company increased its annual sales fivefold.

Source: Adapted from Scarborough, N.M. & Zimmerer, T.W. 1988. *Effective small business management*. 2nd edition. Merrill Publishing: Columbus, p. 483.

Fill in the missing words:

1. The most common way of getting information is through ....

2. Marketing research is the ...., ... and ....
   of marketing information pertaining to the ....,
   ...., or ....

3. One common misconception about marketing research is

   ....

2.1 Identifying/collecting the information that you need

WHAT INFORMATION DO YOU NEED?

One of the secrets of success in marketing research is to think carefully about what information you need and then go about identifying or collecting it. In fact, identifying the information that you need is the first step in marketing research. Think about the decisions that you are going to make and then identify precisely the information that you will need to be able to make those decisions. This is important. Clearly identifying the information you will need for your decisions ensures that you can go out and get that correct information. Do not hurry this step!

Refer below for an example of what is meant by fully understanding what it is that you need information for.

COMMON PROBLEM:
NOT IDENTIFYING THE TRUE PROBLEM

Scarborough & Zimmerer (1988:489) emphasise the importance of clearly identifying the information required. They state:

A common flaw at this stage is to **confuse a symptom with the true problem**. For example, dwindling sales is *not* a problem, but rather a symptom. To get to the heart of the issue, the owner must list all the possible factors that could have caused it. Is there new competition? Are the firm's sales representatives impolite or unknowledgeable? Have customer tastes changed? Is the product line too narrow? Do customers have trouble finding what they want?

STEP I in marketing research: identify precisely what the information is that you need in order to make the correct decisions.

WHAT INFORMATION IS ALREADY AVAILABLE

Once you have decided on what information you need, the next step is to find out what information is already available for you to use. This is called **secondary data or secondary information.**

Secondary information is information that has already been prepared for some other purpose.

This is important, because this information does not cost that much to get, and it may provide the answers that you need.

There are two sources of secondary information or data:
- ❑ internal marketing information
- ❑ external marketing information

INTERNAL MARKETING INFORMATION

The first area to look for this secondary information is **in the business itself**. This is called internal data, because it comes from inside the business. The best place to look is in the business records. For example, by looking at the cheques and sales receipts you may be able to determine the extent of your coverage of an area. Other internal sources of information can include financial statements, salesperson's reports and invoices.

INTERNAL SOURCES OF INFORMATION

- ❑ sales records
- ❑ merchandise and stock control records
- ❑ customer requests
- ❑ invoices
- ❑ records of returns to suppliers or manufacturers
- ❑ customer complaints
- ❑ advertising records
- ❑ customer credit records
- ❑ financial statements
- ❑ salesperson's reports

Source: Hutt, R.W. & Stull, W.A. 1992. *Marketing: an introduction.* South Western: Cincinatti, p. 85.

Internal information is secondary information that exists inside the business.

EXTERNAL MARKETING INFORMATION

The other area for secondary information is information that has been compiled **outside the company**. This is called external information (Anderson & Dobson, 1994:84). Your job is to try to find out exactly what is available and to collect it. It is usually fairly inexpensive to get this information, and it may be enough to help you to make the decision that you need to make.

You need to look carefully at whatever secondary information you get, because you must consider if it is usable. It may not be current, for example, and it is dangerous to make decisions based on out-of-date data. It may not be specifically what you wanted and you may decide that although it is useful it does not really provide the answers that you want. Finally, you need to consider the source of the information, and decide whether or not you can trust it! There are many possible sources of external marketing information, so sit down and try to list the places that you can think of that may have some information that you can use. Start with trade associations, local councils, and government agencies.

SOME SOURCES OF EXTERNAL MARKETING INFORMATION

- ❑ local councils e.g. population studies, development studies
- ❑ government agencies e.g. Board of Trade & Industry
- ❑ central statistical services
- ❑ trade association   e.g. Furniture Manufacturers Association
- ❑ trade magazines   e.g. *Liquor Store Monthly*
- ❑ newspapers   e.g. *Star, Sowetan, Business Day, City Press*.

Source: Adapted from Hutt, R.W. & Stull, W.A. 1992. *Marketing: an introduction*. South Western: Cincinatti, p. 87.

External information is information gathered from outside the business.

Although secondary information is often easy to get, it may not be in the format you need or accurate enough for your needs. **Secondary research has both advantages and disadvantages.**

ADVANTAGES AND DISADVANTAGES OF SECONDARY RESEARCH

Advantages

- ❑ less costly
- ❑ easy to collect
- ❑ gives guidance for primary research

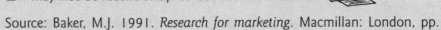

Disadvantages

- ❏ may not be available
- ❏ may not be relevant
- ❏ may not be accurate
- ❏ may not be recent or up-to-date

Source: Baker, M.J. 1991. *Research for marketing*. Macmillan: London, pp. 45-47.

STEP 2 in marketing research: find out what information is already available that you can use.

WHAT INFORMATION WILL I HAVE TO TRY TO GET

Every effort should be made to collect all the secondary information that is available but if it is not enough or not the right information, you will have to get information on your own. This is called **primary data or primary information**.

Primary information is new information collected by the small business person.

There are many ways of getting this primary information. One method is by **observation**. In observation you simply observe the behaviour of the person and note it down. It is an easy method for a small business person to use, and it is inexpensive.

Another method is **personal interviews**. Here you ask the person being interviewed some specific questions face-to-face. This method is very flexible and allows you to adapt your questions to seek out specific answers. However, interviews are often time-consuming and expensive.

Telephone interviews are often used because they are easy and fairly inexpensive. They are not as personal as face-to-face interviews, and do not allow you to make use of visual aids. Also, most people being interviewed do not like to talk for long on the phone.

Mail surveys are another way of getting primary information. They are fairly inexpensive and let the person answering take his/her own time to answer. The time to get information is fairly long and you have very little control as to who answers the questions. Another problem is that not many of the people who receive the mail survey actually bother to answer it.

A further method of gathering primary information is by using a **focus group,** where you bring a group (e.g. 8 to 10 people) together and guide the members in a discussion about a topic. Focus group discussions are fairly fast, easy to do, and inexpensive. They do need a good communicator to run the group.

METHODS OF GETTING PRIMARY DATA – ADVANTAGES AND DISADVANTAGES		
METHOD	**ADVANTAGE**	**DISADVANTAGE**
Observation e.g. in a retail store	❑ good for seeing how customers act ❑ can help in design of product or pack	❑ expensive ❑ no personal contact ❑ relies on what you see – does not say "why"
Personal interviews	❑ can establish contact ❑ can overcome resistance ❑ can choose specific people to answer (e.g. men) ❑ good if asking only a few people ❑ good for getting facts	❑ expensive ❑ time pressure ❑ cannot go too far abroad
Telephone	❑ cheap ❑ can get good response rate ❑ can probe ❑ people don't have to identify themselves ❑ easier to answer questions than if face-to-face	❑ phone can be put down ❑ not much time available ❑ cannot see person answering

METHOD	ADVANTAGE	DISADVANTAGE
Mail surveys	❑ cheap ❑ good coverage ❑ person answering not identified ❑ gives time to think ❑ good where people may be too busy to see you	❑ low number of people reply ❑ little control as to who answers ❑ cannot see person answering ❑ may waste a lot of letters ❑ may have to wait a long time for returned answer
Focus groups	❑ can get people to answer in depth ❑ can see people as they answer ❑ easy to use ❑ fast ❑ inexpensive	❑ need a trained person to run these ❑ must be able to record important aspects

Source: Adapted from Anderson, A.H. & Dobson, T. 1994. *Effective marketing: a skills and activity-based approach.* Blackwell: Oxford, p. 89.

For each of these methods, you will have to make sure that you **prepare the questions** that you will ask. By having the questions prepared and designed so that answers are easy to mark down, you increase the likelihood that people will give you the chance to get the information you need and you reduce the time needed to do it. Sondeno (1985:189) suggests that small business people ask **questions related to the areas of trade, customer preferences and attitudes, and to what would be effective promotion**.

It is important to take care over designing the questions, so that when people answer the questions you will get the information you need. According to Adcock *et al* (1993:125), this means that for your question to be effective, the people answering must:

❑ be able to understand the question
❑ be able to answer the question
❑ be willing to provide the information

You will need to be careful with the questions themselves. Ask short, easy-to-understand questions. Avoid trying to get the person answering to give you the specific answer you wish to get. You must not lead people as to how they should answer, because you want them to give you their own views and answers.

According to Ennew (1993:45), there are usually three types of questions that you can ask:

❑ **Open ended questions**
   Open ended questions mean that the person answering the question can give any answer they want to. This provides useful information, but may make it hard to analyse.

❑ **Either-or questions**
   Either-or questions offer the choice of two answers only, and are good for easy or factual information.

❑ **Multiple choice questions**
   Multiple choice questions provide a number of answer choices and the person must choose which answer he/she wants. This type of question can get information on how people feel and is useful for complex data.

EXAMPLES OF QUESTION TYPES	
TYPE	**EXAMPLE**
Open-ended	Why do you buy this product? ....
Either-or	Are you ☐ Male ☐ Female
Multiple choice – a number of choices possible	Which of the following financial products do you own? ☐ bank current account ☐ bank savings account ☐ building society account ☐ credit card ☐ petrol card ☐ life insurance
Multiple choice – only one answer possible	What is your bank? ☐ Volkskas ☐ First National ☐ Standard ☐ United ☐ Trust Bank Other: specify .... ☞

TYPE	EXAMPLE
Multiple choice – one answer	What was the most important reason for choosing your current bank? ☐ offered best service ☐ good location ☐ recommended by friends ☐ friendly staff

Source: Adapted from Ennew, C.T. 1993. *The marketing blueprint.* Blackwell: Oxford, p. 46.

STEP 3 in marketing research: determine what information you will have to get on your own.

1. Why is it so important to collect/identify information for marketing research? ....
    ....
    ....

2. What value do internal sources of information such as sales records and customer requests have for a small business person with regard to marketing research?
    ....
    ....
    ....

3. Explain the difference between primary and secondary information for marketing research
    ....
    ....
    ....

3.2 Analying the information

Once you have the information that you need you will have to determine what the information means! You need to **organise, summarise and simplify** the information. Use tables, charts, and other visual aids to make it easier to see and understand what the information means.

SUMMARISING AND SIMPLIFYING RESULTS:

Fifty customers of a fast-food outlet were asked what new food offerings they would like the outlet to have for them. The results were as follows:

FOOD TYPE	NUMBER OF RESPONSES	%
Pizza	12	24
Fried Chicken	24	48
Self-help Salads	8	16
Garlic Bread	20	40

The owner of the fast-food outlet decided that he would add both fried chicken and garlic bread to his menu and would send a pamphlet to all his existing customers informing them of this.

STEP 4 in marketing research: organise, summarise and simplify the information.

3.3 Using the information

Small business people often make decisions based only on what they think or feel. With the information available from your marketing research, you will have a sounder basis for making decisions! Be careful that you actually use the information to make decisions regarding operational aspects of your business, such as products offered, prices set, location of the business, messages to use in advertising, and the like. **Remember – the value of information is in its use**. The example above shows that the owner of the fast-food outlet used his information to add two specific items to his menu for his customers. The fact that these were the two most popular requests, as shown by his research, means that they should be good sellers and add to his turnover.

STEP 5 in marketing research: make decisions based on your information.

Marketing research is a process. Can you remember the five steps in this process? Complete the diagram by labelling each box with a step.

```
┌─────────────┐
│             │
│             │
└──────┬──────┘
       │
       ▼
┌─────────────┐
│             │
│             │
└──────┬──────┘
       │
       ▼
┌─────────────┐
│             │
│             │
└──────┬──────┘
       │
       ▼
┌─────────────┐
│             │
│             │
└──────┬──────┘
       │
       ▼
┌─────────────┐
│             │
│             │
└─────────────┘
```

4   ADDITIONAL WAYS TO OBTAIN INFORMATION

One way of checking that your information is accurate is to collect the same information in different ways and to compare the results. For example, you might survey some customers *and* run a few focus groups just to see if the answers and information from the two methods are similar.

SOME SUGGESTIONS ON HOW TO GET INEXPENSIVE INFORMATION

- ❑ Check warranty cards, inventory records, and customer letters to see what goods are gaining or losing popularity.
- ❑ Read industry trade journals (magazines) to keep track of new trends.
- ❑ Set up your own group of customers to tell you how well your company is meeting customer needs.
- ❑ Run some focus groups to gather suggestions for changes to the business.
- ❑ Contact the people who are not customers and find out why.
- ❑ Ask your suppliers about any trends they have spotted.
- ❑ Read publications for important business information.
- ❑ Get customer profiles from local radio stations.
- ❑ Teach all employees to be good listeners and ask them what they have heard.
- ❑ Use a suggestion box.
- ❑ Contact customers who have not bought for a while and find out why.

Source: Adapted from Zimmerer, T.W. & Scarborough, N.M. 1994. *Essentials of small business management.* Macmillan: New York, p. 164.

5 SELF-EVALUATION

5.1 TERMS YOU HAVE LEARNED

(a)   Explain each of the following:

- ❑ marketing research
- ❑ external information
- ❑ secondary information
- ❑ primary information
- ❑ internal data

(b)   Test yourself by matching the term with the correct meaning from the list below. Write your answer in the space provided.

A. Marketing research

B. Secondary information

C. Internal information

D. External information

E. Primary information

QUESTIONS	ANSWERS
1. Secondary information that exists inside the business.	
2. New information collected by the small business person.	
3. Information that has already been prepared for some other purpose.	
4. The collection, analysing and interpreting of marketing information pertaining to your market, customers or competitors.	
5. Information gathered from outside the business.	

5.2 Quiz

(i) Name three commonly used sources of information.

1. .... 2. ....

3. ....

(ii) Give two reasons why small businesses often perform less marketing research than bigger companies.

1. .... 2. ....

(iii) What is the first step in marketing research?

....

....

....

(iv) Name two types of secondary data.

1. .... 2. ....

(v) What three things should you look for in secondary data?

1. .... 2. ....

3. ....

(vi) List 5 ways of getting primary data

1. ....

2. ....

3. ....

4. ....

5. ....

(vii) What are the three important things to consider when designing questions?

1. ....

2. ....

3. ....

(viii) What types of questions can be asked when you design a questionnaire for marketing research?

....

....

....

....

....

....

(ix) Answer the following question by completing the sentence:

The value of marketing information lies in ....

....

....

5.3 Case Study

Below is a survey questionnaire used to get information for a producer of wooden pallets. The questionnaire was used to get information from current users of wooden pallets.

QUESTIONNAIRE

Special note: If you would like to receive information on our wooden pallets once production has started, please check the square below and write in your current mailing address.

I would like to secure this information

Address:...

....

....

---

1   Does your business currently use wooden pallets?   YES

    ....

    (If No, skip to Question 7).

2   What percentage of your wooden pallet needs require **Expendable Pallets** (pallets used only once)?

    0   –   25%   ....

    6   –   50%   ....

    51 –   75%   ....

    76 –   100%   ....

3   For each of the following types of wooden pallets, please indicate the approximate quantity you require each year.

TYPE	QUANTITY
Pallet Bins (all sizes)	....
Pallet boxes (all sizes)	....
Other (please specify)	....

4   Please indicate which one of the following statements best describes your firm's buying patterns for wooden pallets. (Please check only one.)

    Purchase each month   ☐

    Purchase about twice a year ☐

    Purchase only once a year   ☐

5   Approximately how close to your business site is your major supplier of wooden pallets?

    Less than 20 km

    20 –   50 km   ....

    51 –   80 km   ....

    81 –   120 km   ....

    121 –   150 km   ....

    Over 150km   ....

6 What suggestions would you make to help us provide wooden pallets to better meet your needs?

....

....

7 Please indicate the major products of your firm.

....

....

> Please mail the questionnaire back to us in the enclosed self-addressed envelope.
>
> **THANK YOU FOR YOUR CO-OPERATION**

Source: Adapted from Longenecker, J.G., Moore, C.W. & Petty, J.W. 1994. *Small business management: an entrepreneurial emphasis.* 9th edition. South Western: Cincinatti, pp. 194-195.

Answer the following questions after you have read the questionnaire.

1. Why do you think the producer found it necessary to compile the questionnaire?

....

....

....

....

2. Why do you think question 2 was included in the questionnaire?

....

....

....

....

3. Can you think of another question that the producer could have asked the customers?

....

....

....

6 REFERENCES

Adcock, D., Bradfield, R., Halborg, A. & Ross, C. 1993. *Marketing principles and practice*. Pitman: London.

Anderson, A.H. & Dobson, T. 1994. *Effective marketing: a skills and activity-based approach*. Blackwell: Oxford.

Baker, M.J. 1991. *Research for marketing*. Macmillan: London.

Crimp, M. 1985. *The marketing research process*. 2nd edition. Prentice Hall: Englewood Cliffs.

Ennew, C.T. 1993. *The marketing blueprint*. Blackwell: Oxford.

Hutt, R.W. & Stull, W.A. 1992. *Marketing: an introduction*. South Western: Cincinnati.

Longenecker, J.G. Moore, C.W. & Petty, J.W. 1994. *Small business management: an entrepreneurial emphasis*. 9th edition. South Western: Cincinnati.

Scarborough, N.M. & Zimmerer, T.W. 1988. *Effective small business management*. 2nd edition. Merill:Colombus.

Sondeno, S.R. 1985. *Small business management principles*. Business Publications: Plano.

Zimmerer, T.W. & Scarborough, N.M. 1994. *Essentials of small business management*. Macmillan: New York.

3

CHOOSING TO WHOM TO MARKET: PINPOINTING THE TARGET MARKET

1 LEARNING OBJECTIVES

After you have studied this chapter you should be able to:

❑ explain what is meant by market segmentation and target market
❑ explain the advantages and disadvantages of segmentation
❑ choose which approach to segmentation applies to you
❑ segment consumer markets
❑ segment organisational markets
❑ explain the criteria for segmentation to be useful
❑ position your product offering
❑ know the process to follow in order to segment a market

2 INTRODUCTION

In both of the previous two chapters we emphasised the importance of knowing who your customers are and being able to provide a profile of your customers. What if you are thinking of marketing a brand new product or starting up a new business from scratch? Who will your customers be then?

Zimmerer and Scarborough (1994:167) state that one of the principal objectives of market research is identifying the small business's target market. They provide a useful definition of a target market.

A target market is the specific group of customers at whom the business aims its goods or services.

This definition is important, because one of the biggest mistakes made by many small businesses is not being able to define clearly what or who their target market is. To be effective in your marketing you need to be able to give a clear, precise description of who your target customers are. Your **customer profile**, which we explained previously and which can be built up from marketing research, does this for you. This target customer sets the tone for all the marketing decisions that you make. This means that the **marketing mix revolves around the target market and its needs**. Without a clear idea of this target market, the small business person often tries to reach all customers and ends up appealing to almost no-one!

3 MASS MARKETING OR MARKET SEGMENTATION

Hutt & Stull (1992:170) provide a useful definition of a **market**.

> **A market consists of customers who are both willing and able to buy.**

Such a market is made up of either individual **consumers** or **organisations**. For example, if you open a printing shop you may have individual customers who want wedding invitations printed, and you may print business cards for local business organisations.

There are two ways of dealing with markets:
- ❑ mass marketing
- ❑ market segmentation

3.1 Mass marketing

Mass marketing occurs when the small business person aims his/her product at a very **large, broad** market made up of individuals (Hutt & Stull, 1992:171).

For this type of marketing to work, you need a very large group of customers who all want the same thing. If this is the case, then your one and only marketing mix will appeal to all of the customers. Unfortunately, this is seldom the case. It is very difficult to market only one product that appeals to all customers. More and more customers are looking for products that are designed to meet their own specific needs and requirements.

> **Mass marketing means aiming your marketing mix at a large, broad consumer market.**

3.2 Market segmentation

Within the total market, there are often **groups** of people who have **similar characteristics**. These groups are called **market segments** (Hutt & Stull, 1992:171).

The trick is to divide up the total market into these customer groups or segments which have similar characteristics. The process of doing this is called **market segmentation** (Longenecker *et al*, 1994:58).

By segmenting the market, you identify specific groups of customers who will probably respond favourably to a marketing mix which is specifically aimed at their needs. Once you have identified these segments the market segment at which you choose to aim your marketing mix is your **target market**. The target market or markets you decide on will be the ones at which you aim specific marketing prices.

EXAMPLE OF MARKET SEGMENTATION

If you open a business selling personal computers you may decide to segment your market into the following groups:

- ❑ computers for small businesses (invoicing, record keeping)
- ❑ computers for home use (games, financial planning)
- ❑ computers for portable use (laptops)
- ❑ computers for specialised areas (desktop publishing)

In this way as Frain (1994:125) points out, the whole marketing effort is made more effective because:

- ❑ you can develop products that are closely tied in to specific customer needs
- ❑ developing the marketing mix becomes easier

Market segments are groups of customers within the total market who have similar characteristics.

Market segmentation is dividing up a market into several smaller groups with similar needs.

MARKET SEGMENTATION

1 Assume you are opening up a sporting goods store. You have identified two segments of interest: teenagers and middle aged sports enthusiasts. How will you adapt your marketing mix for these two segments?

2 Identify the possible segments for the following two perfume products:
 a high priced, exclusive, unique packaging, advertising emphasises dignity and class
 b low priced, mass produced, standard packaging, advertising emphasises sportiness and freshness

4 ADVANTAGES AND DISADVANTAGES OF SEGMENTATION

What benefits does segmentation offer a small business person?

Marx and Van der Walt (1993:112) identify the following **advantages**:

❑ Segmentation can help you identify excellent **marketing opportunities** when research helps you find a segment that is wide open to you. In the example of personal computers you may have found that there was no-one who had chosen to market to the segment that was looking for specialised areas of application, and this would be an excellent opportunity of which to take advantage.

❑ Segmentation can give you **guidelines as to how to tailor your product offering and marketing mix** for each segment. By having a clear customer profile you know what products to offer to the segment, what their pricing expectations are, how to communicate with that segment, and how to get your product to customers in that segment.

❑ Through segmentation you can **satisfy** your customers better by designing your marketing mix specifically to meet that segment's needs. By doing this you give people in that segment exactly what they want, and this means there is a greater chance that you will satisfy those customers and thus strengthen your business.

Despite all of these benefits, segmentation does have some **disadvantages** for the small business person:

❑ Segmentation can make being in business more **expensive** because the development of separate marketing mixes for each segment means that there will be more marketing costs and effort involved.

❑ The small business person runs the danger of **losing focus** of his/her important markets through proliferating models and producing different variations of the product in an attempt to satisfy too many marketing segments.

In general, we can see that if you use segmentation properly and focus on your important customers, you will gain the benefits of segmentation for your business.

5 THREE APPROACHES TO MARKET SEGMENTATION

A small business has **three options** or **approaches** in terms of dealing with the market and segments. These three approaches are:

❑ **mass marketing approach**
❑ **multi-segment approach**
❑ **concentrated or niche approach**

Although we have already discussed mass marketing and segmentation in general, let's look in more detail at these three approaches, using as an example a small business making leather briefcases.

5.1 Mass marketing approach

As we have already explained, if your small business identifies "everyone" as its target market you are following the **mass marketing approach**. Here you assume that all customers want the same thing and you have **only one marketing mix** aimed at everyone.

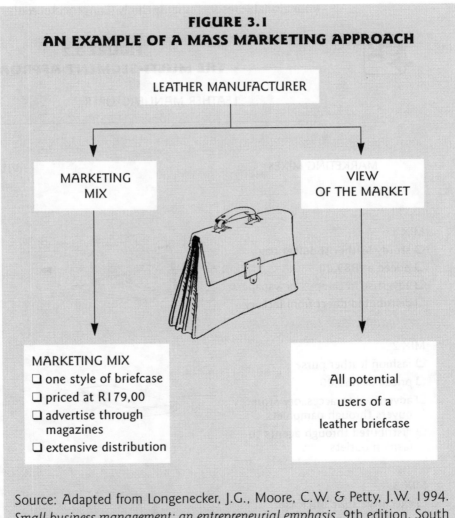

FIGURE 3.1

AN EXAMPLE OF A MASS MARKETING APPROACH

LEATHER MANUFACTURER

MARKETING MIX

VIEW OF THE MARKET

MARKETING MIX
- ❑ one style of briefcase
- ❑ priced at R179,00
- ❑ advertise through magazines
- ❑ extensive distribution

All potential users of a leather briefcase

Source: Adapted from Longenecker, J.G., Moore, C.W. & Petty, J.W. 1994. *Small business management: an entrepreneurial emphasis.* 9th edition. South Western: Cincinatti, p. 60.

If you decide to use the mass marketing approach, you will offer just one type of briefcase, for which everyone will pay R179-00, and this will be communicated by means of a single promotion and distribution plan. In other words, it does not matter what type of customer it is: you treat everyone as if they are the same and they can take it or leave it!

5.2 The multi-segment approach

In terms of the multi-segment approach, the small business identifies **different groups in the market**, and chooses several of these segments which it thinks will be profitable. It will then design **separate marketing mixes** for each segment or target market. Note that the fact that these segments are identified implies that they are different from one another, and that they have different needs.

As shown in the example of the leather manufacturer (in Figure 3.2), the business has identified three distinct market segments: students, females and executives. It has decided to go for all three market segments or target markets, for which it develops separate marketing mixes (mixes 1, 2 and 3). It is clear that there are differences in the marketing mixes aimed at the three chosen target markets. It is important to warn you not to choose too many target markets, as this will spread your available resources fairly thinly (Longenecker *et al*, 1994:62).

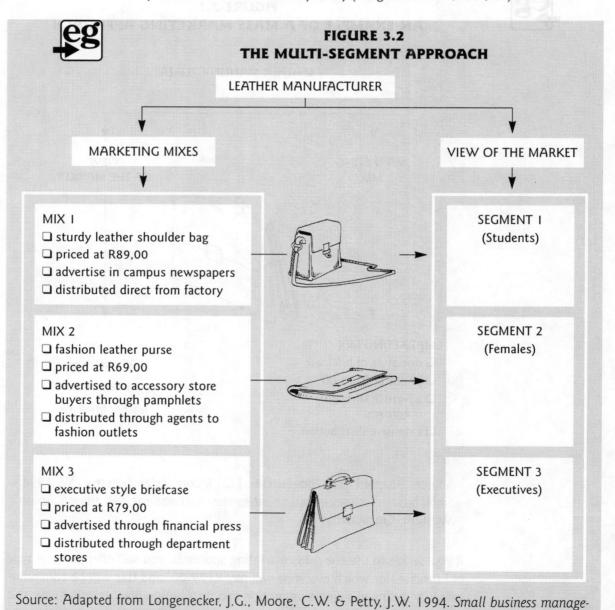

FIGURE 3.2
THE MULTI-SEGMENT APPROACH

LEATHER MANUFACTURER

MARKETING MIXES

VIEW OF THE MARKET

MIX 1
❑ sturdy leather shoulder bag
❑ priced at R89,00
❑ advertise in campus newspapers
❑ distributed direct from factory

SEGMENT 1
(Students)

MIX 2
❑ fashion leather purse
❑ priced at R69,00
❑ advertised to accessory store buyers through pamphlets
❑ distributed through agents to fashion outlets

SEGMENT 2
(Females)

MIX 3
❑ executive style briefcase
❑ priced at R79,00
❑ advertised through financial press
❑ distributed through department stores

SEGMENT 3
(Executives)

Source: Adapted from Longenecker, J.G., Moore, C.W. & Petty, J.W. 1994. *Small business management: an entrepreneurial emphasis.* 9th edition. South Western: Cincinatti, p. 61.

5.3 Concentration or niche approach

In terms of the **concentration or niche approach** the manufacturer will concentrate all his efforts on **one or two small market segments** or niches (Anderson & Dobson, 1994:61). The segment or target market selected will be the one that the manufacturer feels will be the most profitable or that is not adequately served by its competitors. If we go back to the example of the leather manufacturer, he may have decided that he can do best by concentrating only on the executive segment of the market, and he will then choose to implement marketing mix 3 aimed at that segment as illustrated in Figure 3.3.

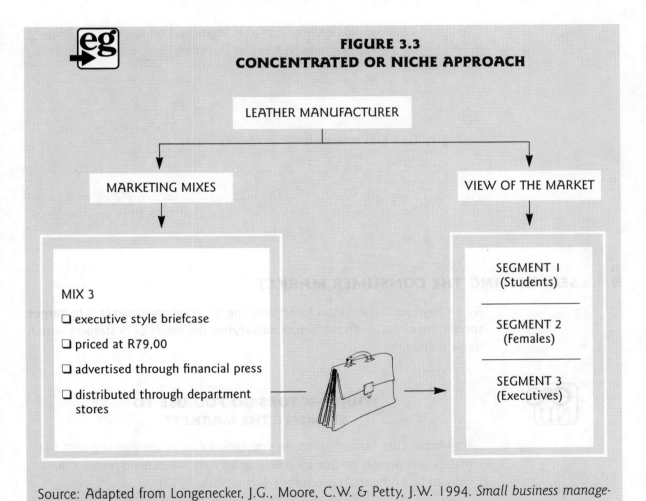

FIGURE 3.3
CONCENTRATED OR NICHE APPROACH

LEATHER MANUFACTURER

MARKETING MIXES

VIEW OF THE MARKET

MIX 3
- executive style briefcase
- priced at R79,00
- advertised through financial press
- distributed through department stores

SEGMENT 1
(Students)

SEGMENT 2
(Females)

SEGMENT 3
(Executives)

Source: Adapted from Longenecker, J.G., Moore, C.W. & Petty, J.W. 1994. *Small business management: an entrepreneurial emphasis*. 9th edition. South Western: Cincinatti, pp. 7–9.

A small business that is just starting should consider following the concentrated or niche approach. This approach allows the start-up business to **specialise** and also **makes better use of scarce resources**. Once the profitability and customer base of the business have been established in the niche the small business person can consider expanding into new markets.

In the example of the leather manufacturer, the business can first target the executive market and, once success is achieved there, can decide whether or not to go for the other two segments(students and females).

1. Name two disadvantages of market segmentation.

    ....

    ....

2. How, on the other hand, might a small business benefit from segmentation? Name three benefits

    ....

    ....

3. (a) What would be the best market segmentation approach to follow for a small business that is just starting?...............................

    ....

    ....

    (b) Give two reasons for your answer in (a).

    ....

    ....

6 SEGMENTING THE CONSUMER MARKET

As we have seen, the reason for segmenting the consumer market is to **target** specific segments, with the aim of **satisfying** the needs of customers within those segments.

WHAT FACTORS DO YOU USE TO SEGMENT THE MARKET?

Any factor that helps distinguish consumers can be used to segment the market and there is no one ideal way to do it. It will depend on your business and its potential customers (Hutt & Stull, 1992).

For example, if you open a leather products store the factors you use to segment the market will be different from those used by someone who opens a furniture manufacturing concern.

There are four broad areas or factors often used to segment consumer markets:

- ❑ **geographic factors**
- ❑ **demographic factors**
- ❑ **lifestyle factors**
- ❑ **customer behaviour factors**

6.1 Geographic factors

When you use geographic factors to segment the market, you divide up the market according to where customers are **located**. It should be clear that there are differences between consumers living in different regions of South Africa and between people living in cities and those living in rural areas. Examples of geographic factors are: the region where customers are, whether they live in a high density or low density area (urban or rural), and, if they live in a town, then the size of the town (large or small). Refer to Figure 3.4 for specific examples of geographic factors.

6.2 Demographic factors

Demographic factors are commonly used by all types of businesses to segment markets. Demographic factors help you to **describe** your customers and tell you who your customers are. Some of the most commonly used demographic factors are: sex, age, marital status, and occupation. Other possible descriptors include family size, income level, ethnic origin and education level. This type of information is usually available from government statistical services and is often fairly easy to obtain. Almost all target markets can be identified with demographic data in combination with some of the other factors, such as lifestyle. Refer to Figure 3.4 for specific examples of demographic factors.

6.3 Lifestyle factors

When you use lifestyle factors to segment the market you divide up the market according to customers' **activities, interests and opinions**. Lifestyle factors give an indication of how people live their lives. To use lifestyle factors, you need to be able to answer questions such as:

❑ How do customers spend their time? (activities)
❑ What things interest prospective customers? (interests)
❑ How do prospective customers see the world around them? (opinions)

Lifestyle factors are more difficult to use than geographic or demographic factors because information on the last two is often readily available to you in secondary sources. Lifestyle information is seldom readily available, however, and you will usually have to find out this information for yourself.

Lifestyle factors are very useful, though, in that they really help you to fine-tune your marketing effort by showing you what is of interest to your customers and what types of information sources they use. Refer to Figure 3.4 for specific examples of lifestyle factors. On the next page is an example of various activities, interests, and opinions which could help establish the customer's lifestyle.

ACTIVITIES i.e. how do customers spend their time?	INTERESTS i.e. what do customers find interesting?	OPINIONS i.e. how do customers see the world around them:
Working	Family	Self-opinion
Pursuing hobbies	Home	Social issues
Attending social events	Career	Politics
Going on holiday	Community issues	Business
Looking for entertainment	Recreation and leisure	Economics
Joining a club	Fashion	Education
Community involvement	Food	Products
Shopping	Media; information;	The future
Playing sports	trends	Culture
	Achievements	

6.4 Customer behaviour factors

When you use customer behaviour factors to segment the market you divide up the market according to how customers **behave** towards the product. This involves asking the following types of questions about the product and the customer:

❑ when do customers buy the product?
❑ what benefit do customers seek?
❑ how much of the product do customers use?

It should be clear that, as a small business, you should probably concentrate your marketing efforts on the heavy users of a product category, because they are the most likely customers to purchase your product. Refer to Figure 3.4 for specific examples of customer behaviour factors.

We have only identified four groups of factors for dividing up the market into segments. The small business person can use any factor or factors that help him/her to identify different groups of customers that act in the same or similar ways. There is no perfect way to segment the market, and you will always need to consider alternative possible ways of doing it. You will also do well to consider how your competitors divide up the market.

FIGURE 3.4
EXAMPLES OF FACTORS USED
FOR SEGMENTING CONSUMER MARKETS

FACTOR	POSSIBLE VARIABLES
1. Geographic	
region	Gauteng, Durban-Pinetown, Cape Peninsula, KwaZulu Natal, remainder of Gauteng
size of city or town	under 10 000, 10 000 to 20 000, 20 001 to 25 000, over 25 000 inhabitants
density	urban, suburban, rural
2. Demographic	
age	under 7, 7 to 13, 14 to 19, 20 to 34, 35 to 49, 50 to 56, older than 65 years
sex	male, female
family size	1 and 2, 3 and 4, more than 4 members
family life cycle	young married couples without children, young married couples with children, older married couples with children, older married couples without children living in, singles
income	under R5 000, R5 001 to R10 000, R10 001 to R15 000, R15 001 to R20 000 to R25 000, more than R25 000 per annum
occupation	professional, technical and clerical employees, employees in sales and related services, etc.
religion	Protestant, Catholic, Muslim, other
social class	upper class, middle class, working class
race	black, white, coloured, Asian
3. Lifestyle	
lifestyle	conservative, liberal
personality	gregarious, authoritarian, impulsive, ambitious
leisure	sports, movies, hobbies

FACTOR	POSSIBLE VARIABLES
4. Customer behaviour	
purchase occasion	regular occasion, special occasion
benefits sought	economy, convenience, prestige
under status	non-user, ex-user, potential user, regular user
usage rate	heavy user, medium user, light user
loyalty status	none, medium, strong, absolute

1. Why is it important for a small business person to segment the consumer market?..
....

2. What factor for segmenting consumer markets will you use to:

   (a) compile a customer profile?..
   ....

   (b) decide on the best location for your target market?...................
   ....

   (c) find out who the heavy, medium, and light users of a product/service are?..
   ....

   (d) find out what customers think of a product/service?.................
   ....

SEGMENTING ORGANISATIONAL MARKETS

What if you aim your product at **organisations**? Do the same factors we identified in Figure 3.4 apply to you? Four possible factors which could be used to segment organisational markets are shown in Figure 3.5. These include:

❑ **geographic factors**
❑ **organisational demographic factors**
❑ **organisational type factors**
❑ **usage factors**

FIGURE 3.5
FACTORS FOR SEGMENTING
ORGANISATIONAL MARKETS

FACTOR	POSSIBLE VARIABLES
1. Geographic	
region	Gauteng, Durban-Pinetown, Cape Peninsula, KwaZulu Natal, remainder of Gauteng Province
location	urban, rural
2. Demographic	
number of employees	1–19, 20-99, 100-249, 250 or over
annual sales	less than R1 million, R1 million to R10 million, R10 million or over
3. Organisational type	
type of organisation	manufacturing, institutional, government, semi-state, military, agricultural, hospital
type of goods	installations, accessories, components, raw materials, supplies, services
4. Usage rate	heavy user, medium user, light user

WHAT CRITERIA DO THE SEGMENTS HAVE TO MEET TO BE USEFUL?

There is no limit to the number of ways a market can be segmented, but for segmentation to be effective and useful for you, the segments you choose should meet a number of criteria (Adcock *et al*, 1993:71) as explained below.

CRITERIA

Big enough	Distinctly separate
Durable	Reachable

❑ **Segments must be large enough**.
The segment must be large enough to give the small business person sufficient return for all the marketing effort put in (Majaro, 1993).

❑ **Segments must be distinctly separate**.
Each segment must be clearly separate from others. In practice, it is really impossible to get perfect segmentation and there will always be some overlap between different segments, but you must try to minimise this (Ennew, 1993:96).

❑ **Segments must be reachable**.
You need to be sure that there are suitable ways both to reach the market with your product and to communicate with the market.

> ❑ **Segments must be durable**.
> You need to be sure that the segment will be around for a while. A segment that is here today and gone tomorrow is not very useful to the small business person.

> 1. How does segmenting organisational markets differ from segmenting consumer markets? ....
> ....
>
> 2. What criteria do the segments have to meet to be useful?...................
> ....
> ....

⑨ POSITIONING YOURSELF IN THE MARKET PLACE

Positioning is a very important aspect of marketing for any small business person. Positioning is designing the marketing mix so that customers in the segment understand and appreciate what the small business stands for in relation to its competitors.

> **Positioning is designing the marketing mix so that your customers in the segment understand and appreciate what your small business stands for in relation to your competitors.**

If you take care in deciding how you are going to position yourself, this positioning will provide the **basis** and **direction** for your marketing mix. It will also give you and your employees a **focus** for what you are trying to do in the market place.

> ### FOR POSITIONING TO BE EFFECTIVE AND USEFUL TO YOU, IT MUST MEET A NUMBER OF CRITERIA:
>
> ❑ your positioning must be **clearly communicated** to the market place
> ❑ your positioning must make you **different** to, and **better than,** other competing products. You can do this through design, size, quality, value for money, service or reliability. (The **competitive edge** we identified in chapter 1 will be a basis for how you position yourself.)
> ❑ positioning takes place in the mind of the customer in comparison with your competition. This means that once you decide on your competitive edge, and position your business on the basis of this, you will have to communicate this to the customer and then **check that he understands and believes it.**

Positioning yourself in the market place follows segmentation and the choosing of target markets.

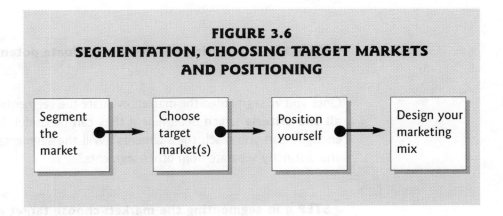

FIGURE 3.6
SEGMENTATION, CHOOSING TARGET MARKETS
AND POSITIONING

In order for you to decide how you will position yourself you will have to know how the competitors are positioning themselves in the segment. You can try to position yourself the same way if you feel you can do better than the competition, or you can find a different position or competitive edge. Just remember, if you decide to position yourself differently to the competition, **you must be different in a way that is important to the customer!** For example, the leather manufacturer we discussed earlier might decide to position itself as the most economical leather briefcase supplier for the executive market.

10 THE PROCESS: HOW DO YOU DO IT?

It should now be clear what steps to follow in order to **segment** the market, to **choose** target markets and to **position** yourself in the market place. Let us go through the steps in this process (Marx & Van der Walt, 1993:123-124).

> **STEP 1 in segmenting the market: analyse the characteristics and needs of potential consumers.**

Firstly, analyse the characteristics and needs of potential customers. Use the information you collect through research to help you to do this. This step will provide you with an indication of the possible factors that you can use to segment the market.

> **STEP 2 in segmenting the market: identify the factors you will use and then segment the market.**

Secondly, decide what factors to use to segment the market. Remember that these might be **geographic, demographic, lifestyle** or **customer behaviour** factors. Remember too that there is no right way of doing this, and you must use the factors to divide up the market into actual segments. Try a number of approaches and decide on the one that you believe works best for you.

STEP 3 in segmenting the market: evaluate potential segments.

Once you've segmented the market, evaluate the segments to see if they **meet all the criteria** which determine if they can be useful. Is the segment large enough? Can you reach the segments? Will the segments last? Is it different and distinctly separate from other segments?

STEP 4 in segmenting the market: choose target markets.

Once you have evaluated the segments, you choose the segment or segments which you believe are right for your business as target markets. Here you will take into account the **potential** of each segment and your **resources,** to determine to how many segments you will be able to market effectively.

STEP 5 in segmenting the market: analyse the competitive position.

The next step is to **evaluate** how your **competitors** are positioning them-selves in the target market(s) you have chosen. How do customers perceive these products? What are your competitors trying to say to their customers? And do you think the customers are being convinced by your competitors and what they are saying?

STEP 6 in segmenting the market: position your product.

Decide how you are going to **position your product** in the target market(s). As stated previously, you might decide to position yourself exactly the same as your competition has and take on the competition head-on. You will only do this, though, if you think your competitive edge is good enough or you believe that the competitors have not really convinced the customers of their posi-tioning.

STEP 7 in segmenting the market: decide on your marketing mix.

Once you have reached this stage you are ready to decide on the marketing mix you want for each target segment. The marketing mix, as we explained earlier, is the **product, price, promotion,** and **distribution decisions** that you will make in order to satisfy the needs of your target market. (In the next four chapters each of these areas will be discussed in detail.)

> **STEP 8 in segmenting the market: monitor your marketing mix and positioning.**

Keep in mind that you need to evaluate your marketing mix and positioning in the target market(s) on a fairly regular basis. You should do this especially when competition increases or new competitors enter the market, or when you feel that change is affecting your customers and/or their needs.

11 SELF-EVALUATION

11.1 Terms you have learned

Explain each of the following?

- ❑ target market
- ❑ market segmentation
- ❑ market positioning
- ❑ multi-segment marketing
- ❑ mass marketing
- ❑ niche marketing

11.2 Quiz

Answer the following questions:

(i)   One of the biggest mistakes made by many small businesses is

....

....

(ii)   Explain two ways in which you can deal with markets

1. ....

2. ....

(iii) Segmentation has some advantages and disadvantages. List them in the box below.

ADVANTAGES OF SEGMENTATION	DISADVANTAGES OF SEGMENTATION
1	1 ....
....	....
2	2 ....
....	....
3	3 ....

(iv) Explain the following approaches to market segmentation:
1. mass marketing approach

....

....

....

2. multi-segment approach

....

....

....

3. concentrated or niche approach

....

....

....

(v) Name some benefits of the concentrated approach for a start-up business.

1. ....

2. ....

(vi) What four factors can be used to segment:
(a) consumer markets?   (b) organisational markets?

(a) 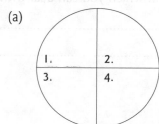   (b)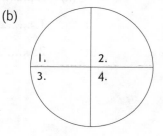

(vii) (a) What is meant by positioning?

....

(b) At what stage (when) does a small business position itself in the market place?

....

....

(c) What three important things must be remembered about positioning?

1 ....

2 ....

3 ....

(viii)

Fill in the eight steps to follow in the segmentation process

STEP 1: ....

STEP 2: ....

STEP 3: ....

STEP 4: ....

STEP 5: ....

STEP 6: ....

STEP 7: ....

STEP 8: ....

11.3 Case study

Baker Street Snacks

Jumping Jack and Diddle Daddle gourmet popcorn brands were launched by Baker Street Snacks in late 1993. Not only has the company created a R100 million popcorn segment, but it has been so successful that the giants like Simba and Willards have decided to follow Baker Street's lead.

Baker Street Snacks, with a brand new factory in Montague Gardens in Cape Town, was established in July 1993 by two ex-Simba directors in conjunction with Cape Town entrepreneur Dave Mostert. Their vision is to dominate the niche snack market in South Africa by developing and manufacturing a range of premium quality gourmet snack brands.

They aim to be low cost producers, while still offering a product that is upmarket and high in quality. Their prime target market was defined as persons aged 18-45 years in the upper income groups, focusing on housewives, and secondly, teenagers aged from 13-18 years.

Source: Adapted from *Professional Marketing Review*, June 1994, p. 57.

Answer the following questions on Baker Street Snacks:

1. What segmentation factors did it use to segment the market?

2. What were the two target markets chosen?

3. Based on its chosen target markets, briefly write down a marketing mix for each target market.

12 REFERENCES

Adcock, D., Bradfield, R., Halborg, A. & Ross, C. 1993. *Marketing principles and practice*. Pitman: London.

Anderson, A.H. & Dobson, T. 1994. *Effective marketing: a skills and activity-based approach*. Blackwell: Oxford.

Ennew, C.T. 1993. *The marketing blueprint*. Blackwell: Oxford.

Frain, J. 1994. *Introduction to marketing*. 3rd edition. Pitman: London.

Hutt, R.W. & Stull, W.A. 1992. *Marketing: an introduction*. South-Western: Cincinnati.

Longenecker, J.G., Moore, C.W. & Petty, J.W. 1994. *Small business management: an entrepreneurial emphasis*. South-Western: Cincinnati.

Majaro, S. 1993. *The essence of marketing*. Prentice-Hall: London.

Marx, S. & Van der Walt, A. (eds.). 1993. *Marketing management*. 2nd edition. Juta: Cape Town.

Professional Marketing Review, June 1994, P. 57.

Zimmerer, T.W. & Scarborough. N.M. 1994. *Essentials of small business management*. Macmillan: New York.

PRODUCT DECISIONS: WHAT EXACTLY DO WE OFFER OUR CUSTOMERS?

4

1 LEARNING OBJECTIVES

After you have studied this chapter you should be able to:

❑ explain what a product is
❑ identify and develop a product mix
❑ describe the different product strategies
❑ choose a suitable brand name for your product
❑ design a good package for your product
❑ describe the implications of warranties
❑ follow the process needed to develop new products

2 INTRODUCTION

Your decisions about your product are extremely important to your marketing. These decisions must be the result of much **thinking, analysis and preparation,** because they will form your "game-plan" to match your small business to the market. They will help you to achieve two things (Adcock *et al*, 1993:153):

❑ **satisfy** the **requirements** of your target market(s)
❑ **meet** your own personal business **objectives**

Adcock *et al* (1993:153) identify a number of reasons why the product decisions you make are so important:

❑ Your product(s) will be the **common factor** linking your business and your customers.
❑ Your product provides the **framework** around which the other components of the marketing mix (price, promotion and distribution) revolve. This means that the decisions you make about your product are central to your marketing effort.
❑ It should be clear that your product will be the **focus of attention** for your customers, as they will be trying to satisfy their needs through the purchase and use of your product.
❑ The product and the delivery of satisfaction to the customer should be the **main objectives of everyone** in your business.
❑ Your product offering will be of **interest** to your competitors, suppliers and potential customers.

This chapter will show you what decisions you need to make in terms of deciding which products to offer to your customers. We will deal with the situation where those products **already exist** (current products) as well as the issue of trying to find **new products** to meet the changing needs of your target markets (developing new products). Before we go any further, however, it is important to understand precisely what a product is.

3 THE PRODUCT CONCEPT

Do you know what a product is? This is not such an easy question because a product can take many forms. It can be a **physical product**, such as leather belts and purses. It can be a **service**, such as panel delivery or a haircutting salon. It can also be a **mix of physical goods and services** such as a hardware store and free advice on building! Each of these things can be termed a product. They all have one thing in common – they are bought by customers to satisfy some need. This helps us to define what a product is (Zimmerer & Scarborough, 1994:179).

> **A product is any item or service that satisfies the need of a consumer.**

Note that customers can differ in their views of what a product is, as it is clear from the above definition that the ideal of "product" has many dimensions. In fact, the product is seen as a mix of some physical features and services, bundled around some benefit that the customer wants (Marx & Van der Walt, 1993:176). This is a multi-dimensional view of a product.

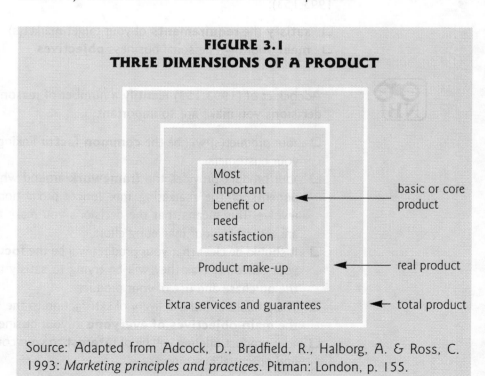

FIGURE 3.1
THREE DIMENSIONS OF A PRODUCT

Most important benefit or need satisfaction → basic or core product

Product make-up → real product

Extra services and guarantees → total product

Source: Adapted from Adcock, D., Bradfield, R., Halborg, A. & Ross, C. 1993: *Marketing principles and practices*. Pitman: London, p. 155.

3.1 Basic or core product

The **basic or core product** is the most important benefit or need satisfaction that your customer expects to get from the product (Marx & Van der Walt, 1993:171).

This is worth noting because customers don't buy products simply for the sake of the product. They buy products because of what that product can do for them, in other words, for the benefit they get from that product. The most commonly used example to illustrate this is the idea of a customer buying a drill bit. What does the customer buy when he/she buys a drill bit for a drill from a hardware store? Does he/she buy just a drill? The answer is no! The essential benefit or basic or core product for the customer is the hole. When someone buys laundry detergent, that person is not simply buying some chemicals, but is buying cleanliness. When someone buys a shoe cleaning service, he/she is buying a well-groomed image, and so on. Your product offering will need to meet this basic need sought by the customer: You will have to identify, in terms of your product or service what the basic need satisfaction or benefit is.

The basic or core product is the essential benefit or need satisfaction that your customer expects to get from the product.

3.2 Real product

The **real product** is made up of the basic product plus all the physical aspects of the product or service offered to the target market (Marx & Van der Walt, 1993:176).

This includes, for example, the design, colour, quality specification, features, styling, brand name and packaging of the product, in other words, all the elements needed to make up the product. Identify what makes up the real product for your product range.

The real product is made up of the basic product or service and all the physical features of that product or service.

3.3 Total product

The **total product** is made up of the basic product, the real product, and all the extras added to the product.

This includes the extra services such as advice, delivery, customer service, warranties and guarantees. An example of the total product, in relation to the basic and real product, can be seen in the example of a men's small tailoring business in Figure 4.2 below.

FIGURE 4.2
THE PRODUCT CONCEPT:
MEN'S SMALL TAILORING SHOP

COMPONENT	DESCRIPTION
❑ Core product	The core product satisfies the need for clothing.
❑ Real product	Clothing consists of material, lining, buttons, zips, a brand name, definite colours, a particular cut and style.
❑ Total product	All the above plus a free fitting service and expert advice on appropriate accessories.

Source: Adapted from Lucas, G. 1986. *The task of marketing management*. Van Schaik: Pretoria, p. 223.

With the increasing competition in most markets, you will be more likely to be successful with your marketing by developing a competitive edge through offering **original service and combinations that make up the total product.** It is at the total product level that you must compete with competitors (Adcock *et al*, 1993:114). It is important that you identify your total product offering and understand how it ties in to your customer needs.

The total product is made up of the basic product, the real product, and all the extras added to the product in terms of service, quality, delivery, or guarantees that are valued by the customer.

What, do you think, are the major benefits for each of the following products/services that customers are looking for?

PRODUCT/ SERVICE	BENEFIT	PRODUCT/ SERVICE	BENEFIT
1. fast food	1.	6. personal computer	6. ....
2. magazine	2.	7. dance lesson	7. ....
3. hair cut	3.	8. shoe repair	8. ....
4. house paint	4.	9. chocolates	9. ....
5. education course	5.		

4 CLASSIFICATION OF PRODUCTS

The small business person needs to decide what type of product he/she is offering to the target market. The type of product you offer affects the way you market it.

There are three major types of products:

❏ **durable products**

Durable products are products that last for some time. This description usually refers to actual products, rather than services. Examples of this type of product are washing machines, lawn mowers and machine tools. They are usually highly priced and are relatively complex products. The fact that they last for some time means that they are not replaced very often.

❏ **non durable**

Non durable products are used up in the short-term. This description usually includes products such as foodstuffs, drinks, household detergent, and nuts and bolts. They are bought fairly frequently and need to be made easily available to the customer. The pricing of these products is usually fairly competitive.

❏ **services**

Services are products that offer instant benefits when the service is performed as opposed to products that involve using, buying or owning. The problem here is that customers cannot see a service, so the challenge for the small business is in showing the value of the service to customers. Examples of services include hair salons, delivery services, auditing services and consultants.

EXAMPLES OF SERVICES	
❑ Accommodation	renting of hotel rooms, flats, guest houses
❑ Household services	repair services for household appliances, cleaning of houses, gardening services
❑ Recreation	cinemas, holiday resorts, video game arcades, sports clubs
❑ Personal services	barbers, beauticians, florists, dry cleaners
❑ Medical services	physiotherapists, dentists, optometrists
❑ Educational services	typing courses, computer courses, small business management courses
❑ Professional services	attorneys, accountants, consultants
❑ Insurance and financial services	insurance brokers, real estate agents
❑ Transport services	taxis, delivery services, transport contractors
❑ Communication services	paging services, cellular phone companies

Source: Adapted from Marx, S. & van der Walt, A. (eds.). 1993. *Marketing management.* 2nd edition. Juta: Cape Town, p. 187.

Products can also be classified and identified according to the people or group at which they are aimed, as follows:

❑ **consumer products** (offered to individual customers), or
❑ **industrial or business products** (offered to other businesses).

4.1 Consumer products

Consumer products are products bought by an individual person for his/her own use.

There are three major types of consumer products, namely **convenience**, **shopping** and **speciality products**. We can decide which of these three types apply to any given product by looking at the customer's behaviour when buying the product:

❑ **convenience products**
Convenience products are products that are purchased frequently. The customer does not make much effort or take long to think about buying convenience products. Examples of convenience products are chocolate bars, soap, toothpaste and coffee. Many of these products are bought on the spur of the moment, such as chocolates, sweets, or magazines, which you often find at the check-out till of supermarkets or cafés. The important aspects of this type of consumer product are that the product must be in stock and easily available to customers.

❑ **shopping products**

Shopping products are products for which customers actually shop around before buying. They compare all the alternatives in terms of price, quality, design and the like. Examples of shopping products are clothing, furniture, and household items such as vacuum cleaners, toasters and kettles. An important aspect of this type of consumer product is that the customers need to know what makes your product different from that of the competitor.

❑ **speciality products**

Speciality products are products that the customer makes a special effort to obtain. Examples of speciality products are exclusive designer clothing, photographic equipment, innovative hi-fi equipment and special coffees. These products are usually only available at selected outlets. An important aspect of this type of consumer product is that it requires that the customer know what makes the product or the place selling the product so "special".

Consumer products are bought by individuals or households for their own personal use.

4.2 Industrial products

Industrial or business products are bought by a business for use in making other products or providing other services (Adcock *et al*, 1993:158).

Examples of different types of industrial products are:

❑ **capital equipment**

Capital equipment is essential equipment/machinery used for, or helping to produce, other products or services. Examples are office equipment, sewing machines and agricultural machines. These products tend to be fairly expensive and last a long time. They usually require fairly high levels of technical knowledge and servicing/maintenance that extend past the time of purchase of the product.

❑ **Materials and components**

Materials and components are products actually used in, or used up in, the making or delivery of the final product. This might be **raw materials** (e.g. potatoes in a fast food outlet serving chips) or **processed materials** (e.g. chemicals used to make paint). Materials – whether raw or processed – usually become part of the product (in other words, they change their form). **Components** also become part of the product but they do not change their form. Examples of components are spark plugs, buttons, and nuts and bolts. These products are usually bought on a contract basis and require some negotiation and assurances of stock and quality.

❑ **Operating supplies**

Operating supplies are products which are used by a business, but not in the manufacturing of the products themselves. Examples are oil, cleaning materials, paperclips and note pads. They are relatively inexpensive, have a fairly short life-span, and are bought without much effort. Important aspects of this type of product are that it must be available to those who want it and it must be competitively priced.

❑ **Industrial services**

Industrial services are those used by a business to support the production process. Examples are office cleaning, catering, waste removal, market research and auditing services. The important aspect of this type of product or service is that the customers need to be made aware of how the service you offer can help them to perform their tasks better and reach their objectives.

Industrial products are bought by a business for use in making other products or services.

IDENTIFY WHAT TYPE OF PRODUCT IS INVOLVED IN EACH OF THE FOLLOWING:	
EXAMPLE	**TYPE OF PRODUCT**
❑ providing homemade sandwiches and snacks to office workers during their breaks	....
❑ designing and installing irrigation systems	....
❑ repairing video recorders and TV sets	....
❑ making executive leather briefcases	....
❑ providing homemade chocolates	....
❑ designing and making matric dance dresses	....
❑ building and repairing wooden pallets	....

Once you know the type of product you will be offering to the target market, the next step is to decide on the product-service mix.

5 THE PRODUCT-SERVICE MIX

The total product offering of a business to the market may be only one item, a number of similar or related items, or a wide variety of very different products. You, as a business person, will have to decide exactly what it is that you will offer your customers.

5.1 The product mix

A product mix consists of all the **product lines** and **product items** that you offer. Let us look in more detail at these terms (Marx & Van der Walt, 1993:177):

❑ **a product line**
A product line is a group within the product mix that contains similar product items. For example, for a men's clothing store the product lines might include shoes, jackets, shirts, trousers, suits and accessories.

❑ **a product item**
A product item is a specific item within a product line. For example, in the suit line for the men's clothing store each individual suit has a specific style and brand name. Each of these individual suits is a product item.

You should be able to see that all decisions made by the small business person with respect to products will always relate to and affect the product items, product lines and product mix:

❑ The more product lines that your business has, the **wider** your product mix

The more product items that you have within a product line, the **deeper** your product line

> **The product mix is the total range of various products that your business makes or sells.**

5.2 The product-service mix

We have previously discussed the idea that a business can offer both products and services. The product-service mix is the **sum of all the products and/or services** offered by a business (Hutt & Stull, 1992:111-114).

Some businesses offer only a pure service (e.g. an insurance broker) and others sell only a product (e.g. cafés). There are many small businesses, however, that offer a combination of products and services (e.g. a painting company that offers both the painting service and the paint it uses).

Hutt & Stull (1992:111) identify four possible product-service mixes:

❑ **complete product**

In the case of a complete product your business does not offer any supporting services at all. Examples of businesses with a complete product are self-service stores, direct mail businesses and stationery stores.

❑ **a product with supporting services**

In the case of a product with supporting services your business offers products that need some services to make the total product of value to your customers. Many of these products are fairly complex and need the help of good salespeople to sell them. Examples of these products are office equipment, expensive clothing, computer equipment, stereo equipment and home appliances. The supporting services often take the form of warranties, installation services, repair services or alterations. The combination of the product and the supporting services will help customers to decide whether to deal with you or with a competitor!

❑ **a service with supporting products**

This is the case where the service offered has to have supporting products in order to be of value. Examples are car repair (requiring parts), hair styling salons (requiring shampoos and gels) and veterinarians (requiring medicines).

❑ **complete service**

In the case of a complete service, no supporting products are needed. Examples are crèches, babysitting services, and investment consultants who provide only a service.

A product-service mix is the sum of all the products and/or services offered by a business.

5.3 Factors affecting your product mix

There are a number of factors which will affect what your product mix looks like (Marx & Van der Walt, 1995:190-195).

These factors include:

❑ **your overall business objectives**

Your objectives in terms of profits and market share will affect how wide your product mix is. If you want to be seen as the product leader, for example, this will imply that you need a broad and deep product mix.

❑ **changes in the market place**

Your customers may be affected by changes in their own circumstances. This may mean that they look for cheaper or more expensive products, or even different type of products. You must know the changing needs of your customers in order to know what changes you may need to make to your product mix. For example, if it becomes trendy for students to wear shoulder bags to carry books and you are a supplier of student school cases then you may have to broaden your product mix by adding a range of shoulder bags.

❑ **competitors' actions**

You may decide to make your product offering different from that of your competitors. You may also add products where the competition is not so strong.

❑ **production considerations**

You may be able to make more efficient use of your production facilities by adjusting your product mix, especially if you have finances and spare production resources to allow you to do so. For example, a manufacturer of leather briefcases might expand his/her product mix by making leather belts on the machinery during the time when there is no demand for briefcases.

1. Into which category of the product-service mix do the following fall:

EXAMPLE	PRODUCT-SERVICE MIX
landscaping services	....
garden services	....
selfserve vegetable shop	....
graphic artist	....
computer consultant	....
TV repair shop	....

2. How will a small business person's objectives with regard to market share and profit affect his/her product mix?

....

....

3. Why is it important for a small business person to be aware of the changing needs of customers?

....

....

6 PRODUCT DECISIONS

What are the types of decisions that a small business person can make in relation to the marketing mix? A number of possible choices are available and may be summarised as follows (Marx & van der Walt, 1993:177-179):

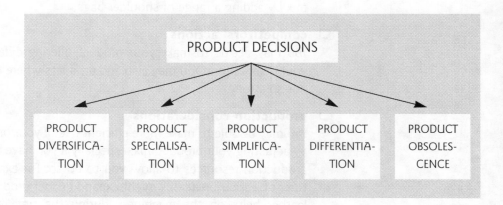

PRODUCT DECISIONS

PRODUCT DIVERSIFICATION · PRODUCT SPECIALISATION · PRODUCT SIMPLIFICATION · PRODUCT DIFFERENTIATION · PRODUCT OBSOLESCENCE

□ **product diversification**
Product diversification is the process of **expanding** the product mix by adding new product items or product lines to the existing mix. For example, a leather manufacturer who makes executive briefcases and women's purses might diversify by making men's leather belts.

□ **product specialisation**
Product specialisation is the process of **eliminating** some product items or product lines from the product mix. For example, a pharmacy selling cosmetics, perfumes and medicines may decide to specialise by selling only medicine and women's perfumes.

□ **product simplification**
Product simplification is the process of **limiting** the shape, sizes or appearance of certain products. For example, a manufacturer of overalls may decide to make only four sizes, three colours and three styles of overall.

❑ **product differentiation**

Product differentiation is the process of trying to **make your product different** from the competitor's products in the eyes of the customers in the target market. For example, a seamstress may decide to differentiate herself from her competitors by using imported material and fully lining all the dresses and jackets she produces.

❑ **product obsolescence**

Product obsolescence is the process of developing new products to **last a specific time** physically or psychologically. In physical obsolescence the product is planned to wear out – for example, a pair of sandals that is designed to last three years. In psychological obsolescence the product does not actually wear out but a new model or style makes it old or outdated – for example, when a new style men's suit comes out the old suit is still useful but becomes outdated or out of fashion.

BRANDING AND TRADEMARKS

Branding and trademarks are used to identify products in the market place. Hutt & Stull (1994:106) give a useful definition of a brand.

A brand is a name, sign, symbol, design or combination of these which identifies a product or service.

Why do business people use brands? Brands are used to **differentiate** the products or services of one business from its competitors. In other words, you use branding to identify your product or services for your customer. Secondly, when you build a good reputation for a brand it makes it easier for you to introduce a new product or service to the market by using the same name. This is called **brand extension**.

Brand extension is when a business uses an existing brand name to help with the introduction of new products.

A **trademark** is a brand or part of a brand that has been granted legal protection (Hutt & Stull, 1994:107).

The business that has registered the trademark gets exclusive use of that trademark, and no competitor is legally allowed to make use of it. Examples of trademarks are Nike, Mamma's Pies, and Coca-Cola. There are legal implications for the small business person registering a trademark, but if you have a good brand name you must register it to protect it.

A trademark is a brand that has been granted legal protection.

69

7.1 Types of brands

There are many types of brands that the small business person can decide to use (Hutt & Stull, 1994: 107-109). Firstly, there is a choice between a **national brand** and a **private brand**:

> ❑ **national brand**
> In the case of a national brand the brand of the manufacturer is sold **nationally** (in other words, across South Africa). Examples of national brands are Busby leather goods, Coca-Cola and Ray-Ban Sunglasses.
>
> ❑ **private brand**
> In the case of a private brand products are **sold under a brand name created by a retailer**. For example, you may be a producer of men's t-shirts and you supply Woolworths. The t-shirt will be sold under the Woolworths label, which is the private brand of Woolworths.

Secondly, there is a further choice between a **family** brand and an **individual** brand:

> ❑ **family brand**
> For the family brand the seller uses the same brand on all its products. For example, the leather manufacturer selling under the Busby leather goods name uses Busby for all its leather products.
>
> ❑ **individual brand**
> For the individual brand the product is known by its own name instead of by the name of the company making the product. For example, Castle, Lion and Hansa are all examples of individual beer brands, all made by SA Breweries.

7.2 Importance of brands

Brands are important for both **customers** and **marketers** (Marx & van der Walt 1993:240-241). For **marketers**, brands provide the following **advantages**:

> ❑ they are the **basis** of advertising and merchandising, as you can make customers aware of the brand and also get them to recognise it.
>
> ❑ they **protect** the marketer from other sellers substituting similar products with your product.
>
> ❑ they make it difficult for customers to **compare** prices because the products are not the same.
>
> ❑ they allow the marketer to **expand** or diversify the product mix.

☞

For **customers**, brands provide the following **advantages:**

- ❑ they **identify** the product at the point of sale
- ❑ they imply a reliable **level of quality** since all products with the same brand name should have the same quality level
- ❑ they **identify the manufacturer** of the brand
- ❑ they can serve as a **warning** to customers if the product did not previously meet their expectations!

7.3 Guidelines for choosing a brand name

There are a few general guidelines that the small business person should keep in mind when choosing a brand name (Longenecker, 1994:319-320):

- ❑ choose a name that is **easy** for the target market **to pronounce**
- ❑ try to choose a name that is **suggestive of the major benefits** of the product
- ❑ use a name for which you will be able to get **legal protection**
- ❑ try to choose a name that **can be used on several product lines**
- ❑ the name should be **original**
- ❑ choose a name that indicates **high quality**

1. Explain the difference between a brand, a brand extension and a trademark by completing the following:

A BRAND	A BRAND EXTENSION	A TRADEMARK
....	....	....
....	....	....
....	....	....

2. Explain what a private brand is. Give an example.

....

....

3. When would you use an individual brand name for a product?

....

....

8 PACKAGING

Once you have decided on a brand name you need to consider how you will package your product.

Packaging is very important, because many products rely only on their pack to attract attention to themselves when sitting on the shelf next to competitive products. In the case of many products, when you think of them, you think of the packaging more than the product itself. Think of toothpaste: the chances are that you imagine the box the product comes in rather than the toothpaste tube itself.

Packaging is the design and production of the container of the product item so that it can be **protected, stored, handled, transported, identified** and **marketed** successfully.

PURPOSE OF PACKAGING	
TASK	**DESCRIPTION**
Enclosement and protection	facilitates the safe and easy despatching
Communication	communicates a specific product image through its design, label, colour, trade-mark and display.
Market segmentation	selection of a specific package design allows your business to direct its products to specific market segments
Co-operation with distribution channels	packaging must satisfy the need of those who store and sell your product

Adapted from Marx, S. & van der Walt, A. (eds.). 1993. *Marketing management.* 2nd edition. Juta: Cape Town, p. 248.

Packaging is the design and production of the container of the product item so that it can be protected, stored, handled, transported, identified and marketed successfully.

8.1 Types of packaging

The small business person must decide what type of packaging to use for his/her products. A number of choices are available (Marx & van der Walt, 1993:249-252).

Types of packaging include:

❑ **family packaging**

In the case of family packaging all the products in the product mix have more or less the same packaging, for example, a range of shampoos and conditioners with very similar packaging.

❑ **individual packaging**

In the case of individual packaging each product gets its own special pack. This helps to give the product an image of exclusivity. For example, a wine maker may choose a separate bottle and label design for each of his/her wine products.

❑ **reusable packaging**

In the case of reusable packaging the packaging is deliberately designed to be used for another purpose once the contents have been used up. For example, a cake bakery may package its cakes in reusable plastic containers with lids that can be sealed.

❑ **multiple packaging**

In the case of multiple packaging several similar product items are packaged together. For example, the bakery mentioned above may package cupcakes in groups of half a dozen.

Multiple packaging can help the small business person to introduce a new product or it can be used to give customers a special deal if they buy in quantity.

Imagine you have decided to open up a German bakery offering special made-to-order cakes and pies. Think of examples of ways you can use each of the different types of packaging mentioned above.

❑ family packaging: ....
❑ individual packaging: ....
❑ reusable packaging: ....
❑ multiple packaging: ....

9 WARRANTIES

A warranty is simply a promise that a product **will do certain things** or **meet certain standards** (Longenecker *et al*, 1994:321). A warranty can be **written** or **verbal**, or **may be implied**.

When will you use a written warranty? Some business people think a written warranty is not always needed, and that it may confuse customers or make them suspicious that the product is not as good as it seems! Warranties are, however, important for certain types of products:

❏ For **innovative products** a warranty will reduce the risk of using a totally new product.

❏ For a **relatively expensive product** a warranty will reduce the economic risk of the product not performing.

❏ For a product that is **complex to repair** a warranty will serve to assure the customer that he/she will not be left with a product that cannot be fixed.

❏ For a product **positioned as high quality** a warranty will serve to underline the image of quality, the warranty being part of the total product that the customer buys.

In deciding whether or not to have a warranty, or the extent of the warranty, the small business person needs to consider the following factors:

❏ the costs of giving the warranty

❏ the capability actually to provide the service he/she is guaranteeing

❏ the competitor's warranties

❏ the expectations of the target market

Care needs to be taken because when warranties are expressly stated this has legal implications.

A warranty is a promise that a product will do certain things or meet certain standards.

10 DEVELOPING NEW PRODUCTS

For all businesses new product development is a critical aspect of making product decisions. New product development is one of the key methods that a small business can use to try to ensure that it has a future. New products are the **lifeblood** of a business. You can, for example, enter new niche segments by developing new products to meet their specialised needs, thus increasing the chances of success for your business.

10.1 Types of new products

New products include a number of types. These range from totally new products (i.e. innovations) to variations on and improvements to existing products.

There are basically three broad types of new products (Adcock *et al*, 1993:181):

❑ **major innovations**

Major innovations are totally new products involving new combinations of technology, new formulations or new user benefits. This type of totally new product is fairly rare and involves quite a large element of risk for the small business person. An example of a  major innovation would be a never-seen-before putty for glueing metal to metal that hardens immediately, developed by an adhesives and glue manufacturer.

❑ **product improvements**

Product improvements involve improving the existing product either slightly or substantially. This could take the form of product re-design, re-packaging, or formula or ingredient changes. For example, the German bakery might decide to improve its chocolate  cakes by using a new processed flour that retains the freshness of the cake for a longer period of time.

❑ **product additions**

Product additions are simply products that are imitations of existing products, or line extensions of products that the small business person is already marketing successfully. For example, the German bakery  might decide to add carrot cake and Black Forest cake to its already successful line of cakes.

10.2 New product development process

The way to develop a new product will vary from business to business, but in general there are several steps that should be followed. These are shown in Figure 4.3. Note that the model looks like a funnel. This is because, of the many ideas that you develop, only a few products will reach the stage where you launch them onto the market!

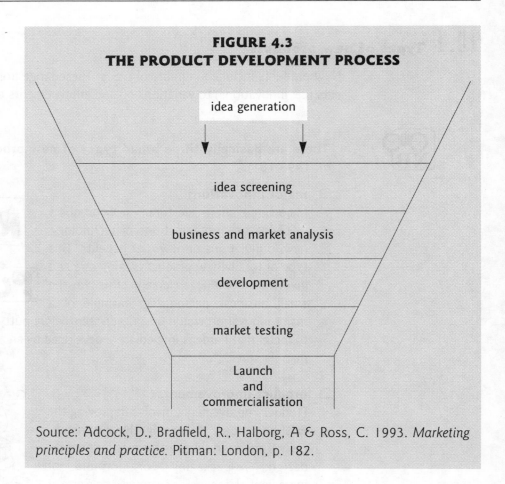

FIGURE 4.3
THE PRODUCT DEVELOPMENT PROCESS

idea generation

idea screening

business and market analysis

development

market testing

Launch
and
commercialisation

Source: Adcock, D., Bradfield, R., Halborg, A & Ross, C. 1993. *Marketing principles and practice*. Pitman: London, p. 182.

(a) Generating ideas

The first step is to generate ideas for possible new products. Obtaining ideas for new products must be an ongoing activity for all businesses, big or small, and part of your research programme. Product ideas can come from **sources outside** the company (customers, competitors) and **inside** the company (employees).

POSSIBLE SOURCES OF NEW PRODUCT IDEAS

INTERNAL	EXTERNAL
❑ your own research and experimentation	❑ competitors' products
❑ your own manufacturing process	❑ customer feedback
❑ market research	❑ customer complaints
❑ salespeople	❑ customer suggestions
❑ customer service activities	❑ outside specialists e.g. research houses, consultants
❑ managers in the business	❑ supplier suggestions
❑ employee suggestions	❑ overseas trends
❑ staff meetings to think of new products	

(b) Screening ideas

Once you have generated ideas, screen or filter the ideas to see which ones are really offering business prospects for you. You need to **rate and rank the ideas** in terms of how well the idea fits with your company, and in terms of your material and financial resources, and marketing capabilities. The idea is to choose those products that show the most potential for your business.

IDEA SCREENING CRITERIA	
❑ business objectives	❑ marketing capabilities
❑ financial capabilities	❑ manufacturing capacity
❑ fit with other products	❑ availability of materials

(c) Analysing the business and the market

At this stage you really **analyse and check the idea**, because if it goes beyond this step, you will have to start spending money in order actually to develop the product.

You will need to do **research** as to what the product should look like, how customers will use the product, and what it will do for customers. You will also need to determine how big the market for the product is, who the customers will be, what the possible prices and profit margins are, and who the competition will be. You will also have to do some **financial planning** in terms of cash flows, costs and profit projections. As we have said, take care to do a good job here, because if you decide to continue, you will start incurring costs.

(d) Development

At this stage you develop an **actual model or sample of the product** (Sondeno, 1985:206). The important task here is to ensure that the model is developed **according to customer needs**. You need to test the product being developed through research with customers, in order to fine tune the product so that it maximises satisfaction of customer needs. You will also need to ensure that the product actually performs. For example, if you design a new trolley to carry heavy objects you will have to test it to ensure that it can withstand heavy weights and can move the weight around without breaking. The more input that potential customers have into the development of the product the greater likelihood of a successful outcome.

(e) Testing the market

Once the product is developed, you may want to check everything by testing the product under market conditions before launching it onto the market. You may choose a small area to use as a test-market area, offer the product to customers, and implement the marketing mix you intend to follow. You will then evaluate and fine tune the marketing mix and see how customers react to the product and the marketing mix. The **advantage** of this approach is that you can **make small changes** to your mix and/or product before launching it fully to your target market. The **disadvantage**, however, is that your **competition might find out** what you intend doing in which case you will lose the element of surprise.

For industrial products, test marketing is often done by means of a trial with a selected customer. Again, the objective is to see the product in the field and make final adjustments.

Some small business people prefer to avoid this step because of the danger of a competitor copying their product and the business losing its advantage of being first to the market or even perhaps being the only one offering the product.

(f) Launching the product

At this stage you launch the product fully onto the market. It is important to plan your launch carefully, **based on your marketing resources** and **capabilities**.

You may want to introduce the product onto separate areas of the market so as to be able to handle the product introduction and marketing, and the orders and demand for the product. Whether or not you follow this route will depend on your evaluation of your resources, capabilities and competition's possible responses. Whichever route you follow, you will have to ensure that you monitor customers' reactions to the new product to make sure everything goes smoothly.

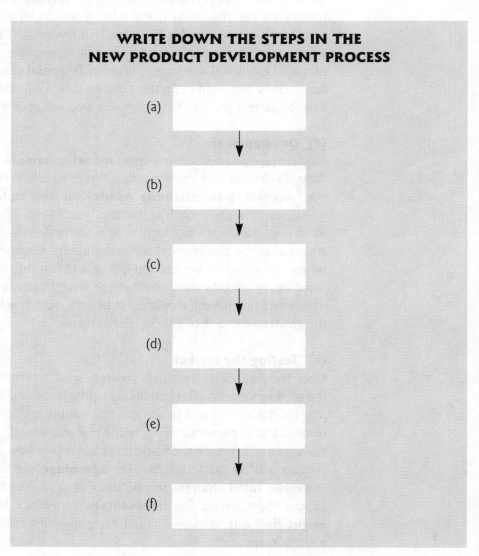

WRITE DOWN THE STEPS IN THE NEW PRODUCT DEVELOPMENT PROCESS

(a)

(b)

(c)

(d)

(e)

(f)

11 SELF-EVALUATION

11.1 Terms you have learned

Explain each of the following:

- ❑ product
- ❑ basic product
- ❑ real product
- ❑ total product
- ❑ trademark
- ❑ consumer product
- ❑ industrial product
- ❑ product mix
- ❑ brand

11.2 Quiz

Answer the following questions

(i) Why are product decisions important?

....

....

(ii) Name three types of consumer products and four types of industrial products.

CONSUMER PRODUCTS	INDUSTRIAL PRODUCTS
1.	1. ....
2.	2. ....
3.	3. ....
	4. ....

(iii) What are the four options for a product-service mix?

1.	2.
3.	4.

(iv) List and briefly explain five different types of product decisions.

1. ....

2. ....

3. ....

4. ....

5. ....

(v) What are the advantages of brands to marketers and customers?

MARKETERS	CUSTOMERS
1.	1. ....
2.	2. ....
3.	3. ....
4.	4. ....

(vi) Why is it important that an expensive lawnmower have a written warranty? ....

....

(vii) Name two sources of ideas for developing new products and give some examples of each. Answer the question by completing the diagram:

SOURCES OF NEW PRODUCT IDEAS	
SOURCE 1	SOURCE 2
EXAMPLES	EXAMPLES
1.	1. ....
2.	2. ....
3.	3. ....
4.	4. ....

11.3 CASE STUDY

EASY WAVES COMPANY

The Easy Waves Company was formed in February 1985 in response to the rapidly growing, but mainly grassroots type, demand for hair products. The initial focus of the company was Johannesburg, concentrating on the then PWV area.

Initial research focused on establishing what trends would influence the market. Along with the rapid urbanisation of the black population was the fact that the demographic profile of the white population is ageing while the black population has a younger profile. This is important, as the cosmetic/haircare market is aimed at the younger sectors of the market. This, tied to the growing disposable income and spending power of the black consumer, positively influenced the entry of Easy Waves into the market place.

Along with the growing affluence of the black consumer was a growing trend towards sophistication and a rise in the aspirations of that target market. This trend was most vividly illustrated by the new and individual "Afro" hairstyles and, more particularly, the wet-look perm. It is not surprising to note that these styles were inspired by black American hairstyles. Black Americans serve as role models and are an important reference group to the emerging black urban consumer in South Africa. In fact, a number of black consumers insist on using very expensive, imported American products.

SELECTING THE TARGET MARKET

The next task for the Easy Waves company was to select a target market for its products. After considerable research into the black haircare market, and keeping in mind the trends already mentioned, the following target market was chosen:

Demographics
Urban black females, aged 18-35 years, in the A, B and C income groups.

Psychographics
Aspirational, very aware of fashion trends, influenced by innovators and movers, for example singers and television news broadcasters. Research revealed that consumers were looking for effective products, but that the primary emphasis on the part of consumers was 'a statement of image', that is, the feeling and the look that comes with effective hair care.

PRODUCT DEVELOPMENT

In considering the actual product to be developed, the characteristics of black hair had to be established and considered. Among the facts that influenced the development of the final product were:

- Black hair is fragile and dry.
- Dry hair lacks natural oils.
- Black hair often grows at an angle against the scalp, which is why the hair strand is very curly.
- The most popular style with the black consumer is the curly perm. The active ingredient in any perm is extremely drying and if the hair is not continuously moisturised breakage is inevitable.
- Moisturisers such as gels and sprays are essential to replenish the natural oils that are stripped from hair following perming.
- Too little moisturising will cause hair breakage; too much leaves hair greasy and clogs the pores of the scalp.

The product concept eventually developed by Easy Waves management was: "products that satisfied consumers' needs for permed hair and shiny, soft, healthy curls and waves".

In line with this was the initial decision to concentrate on the "perm" segment of the black haircare market, particularly products that perm and maintain the hair. This segment constituted approximately 47 per cent of the total black haircare market.

A contract cosmetic and toiletry manufacturer with a good reputation was approached to develop trial formulations of the envisaged products. A product brief was provided, based on the factors listed above, and concentrating on the consumer needs which the products had to satisfy. The product was tested over a six month period that involved qualitative research with consumers as to their attitudes to the product following its usage.

BRANDING AND PACKAGING

The management of the company felt that one of the keys to a successful product is developing a strong, visible brand name and appropriate packaging. Choosing the brand name was the first challenge. An attempt was made to focus on the benefit to the consumer in a fairly literal and direct manner, and after careful consideration of a number of alternatives the final choice was made. The result was the Easy Waves brand name, and its powerful visual logo.

The combination of the brand name and logo clearly illustrated what the product was and, more importantly, what it would do. This is important as, despite rapid urbanisation, the traditional influence in the target market is strong and a substantial number of black consumers are either illiterate or semi-literate, or very literal in their translation of English. (English was identified as the primary language in which to communicate, as the target market most readily identified with it.) The influence of American role models helped to establish English as the language of preference. The name and logo was displayed on the packaging of all products in the Easy Waves range.

The second challenge was packaging. This is extremely important for creating a strong and visible identity for any product. Easy Waves's management tried to:

❑ develop packaging that would not only be appealing to the target market, but would also have an association of quality and value; and
❑ develop distinctive packaging in a market that was rapidly becoming very competitive, with shelf presence as a priority as space in retail outlets came under pressure.

The actual pack shapes chosen were fairly standard. The colours, however, were distinctive: burgundy for the background and lilac for the printing. The initial positive response was substantiated in focus group research, as well as later in quantitative research which revealed the increasing popularity of the products. The product and packaging were now ready for introduction to the market.

Source: van der Walt, A. & Machado,R. (eds.). 1992. *New marketing success stories*. Southern: Johannesburg, pp. 83-86.

Answer the following questions:

(i)   What was the target market chosen by Easy Waves?

(ii) What was the basic need that the Easy Waves product met for its target customers?

(iii) What factors affected the choice of a pack for Easy Waves?

(iv) What method did Easy Waves use to develop its product?

12 REFERENCES

Adcock, D., Bradfield, R., Halborg, A. & Ross, C. 1993. *Marketing: principles and practice.* Pitman: London.

Hutt, R.W. & Stull, W.A. 1992. *Marketing: an introduction.* South-Western: Cincinnati.

Longenecker, J.G., Moore, C.W. & Petty, J.W. 1994. *Small business management: an entrepreneurial emphasis.* 9th edition. South-Western: Cincinnati.

Lucas, G.(ed.). 1986. *The task of marketing management.* Van Schaiks: Pretoria.

Marx, S. & van der Walt, A.(eds.) 1993. *Marketing management.* 2nd edition. Juta: Cape Town.

Sondeno, S.R. 1985. *Small business management principles.* Business Publications: Plano.

Zimmerer, T.W. & Scarborough, N.M. 1994. *Essentials of small business management.* Macmillan: New York.

van der Walt, A. & Machado, R. (eds.). 1992. *New marketing success stories.* Southern: Johannesburg.

PRICE:
5 HOW TO DETERMINE
WHAT TO CHARGE

1 LEARNING OBJECTIVES

After you have studied this chapter you should be able to:

- ❑ define what is meant by price
- ❑ identify the factors affecting price
- ❑ explain the objectives of pricing
- ❑ describe the three basic pricing strategies
- ❑ discuss the various pricing adjustments
- ❑ evaluate decisions regarding the use of credit

2 INTRODUCTION

Pricing is one of the really crucial elements of the marketing mix (Majaro, 1993:93). Pricing affects the chances of long-term success for a small business because of its implications for profit. The significance of pricing lies in the fact that price is the one element in the marketing mix that **brings in revenue**, while the other three elements (product, promotion, distribution) are **costs** (Frain, 1994:176).

Hutt & Stull (1992:288) provide a useful definition of price.

> **Price is the exchange value of a product or service, usually stated in terms of money.**

As stated by Van der Walt *et al* (1995), the price of a product plays **two major roles** in marketing for a small business person:

- ❑ it influences **how much** of a product customers purchase
- ❑ it influences whether selling the product will be **profitable**

As we mentioned in the definition above, price is usually stated in money terms.

However, many small businesses often **exchange goods or services** with each other. This is called **bartering**. In this situation the small business person offers to pay for a product or service with some of his/her own products or services instead of money. For example, a small building contractor may get his bookkeeper/auditor to do his books in exchange for some improvements to the bookkeeper's home.

Bartering is where businesses exchange goods or services with each other.

There are many different forms of price.

FORMS OF PRICE	
TERM	**WHAT IS GIVEN IN RETURN**
price	product or service
tuition fee	education
rent	place to live
interest	use of money
fee	professional services
fare	transport
toll	use of roads
rate	hotel rooms
dues	membership
commission	salesperson's services
salary	work (monthly)
wage	work (hourly)
bribe	illegal actions

Source: Adapted from Van der Walt, A., Strydom J.W., Marx, S. & Jooste, C.J. 1995. *Marketing management*. 3rd edition. Juta: Cape Town. p. 420.

2.1 Different ways of looking at price

One of the important things for any business to consider is the difference between suppliers and customers in the views of price (Majaro, 1953:99). The **supplier** or business person tends to look at price in terms of **costs, volume sold** and **profit margins**. The customer, on the other hand, sees price as something to compare between competing products. This means **customers** think in terms of **benefits gained, needs met and affordability.**

TWO VIEWS OF PRICE	
CUSTOMER	**SUPPLIER**
benefits	costs
needs	volume
affordability	profits

To be successful the small business person will have to address the issue of price from both these points of view!

2.2 Price and non-price competition

Small businesses can compete with one another on the basis of price or on a non-price basis (Hutt & Stull, 1992:385).

Price competition occurs when businesses stress their **low prices**. This means that, if you decide to compete on this basis, you need to respond quickly to any changes in your competitors' prices. The disadvantage of competing on the basis of price only is obvious: competitors can easily match or even beat your price and this strategy is easily copied. It is especially dangerous for a small business to compete only on the basis of price when the business has larger competitors. They may easily be able to undercut the price of the small business because of better volumes, lower costs, or better negotiation power. Most importantly, the larger competitors may be able to maintain the low price longer than a small business. The recent example of US Air airline going under is an example of this: South African Airways reacted to the cut price air fares by undercutting the other airline's price and holding the price down indefinitely.

Non-price competition occurs when small businesses emphasise **competitive edges** other than price to distinguish themselves from their competition. This might be through branding, packaging, service or any factor other than price. This means that you must make customers aware of the competitive edge and convince them that you are worth the difference in price. Keep in mind that whatever choice you make regarding **price** versus **non-price competition,** you will still have to **keep a close eye on the prices of your competitors**!

Fill in the missing words:

1. Price is the element in the marketing mix that brings in .... while the other three elements, namely .... , ... and .... are ....

2. Price is the .... of a product/service, usually stated in terms of ....

3. Bartering is where businesses exchange ....

4. Price competition occurs when businesses emphasise their ....

5. Non-price competition occurs when businesses emphasise .... through service or .... or ....

3 FACTORS AFFECTING PRICE

Deciding on your price is a fairly complex process because of the many factors that influence the price (Ennew, 1993:173-178). The first step, then, in setting your price is to consider these factors. They include:

- ❑ costs
- ❑ competition
- ❑ type of product or service
- ❑ image
- ❑ supply and demand
- ❑ environmental factors

3.1 COSTS

The cost of raw materials is often beyond your control, yet it is a factor which affects all businesses. If your costs are **increasing** you have several options:

- ❑ pass increases on to customers
- ❑ pass some of the increases on and absorb others
- ❑ stop selling the product

For example, when vegetable costs increase the higher prices are often passed on by vegetable and fruit vendors to their customers.

What happens when costs **decline**? Here you have two choices:

- ❑ reduce your selling price and keep profits the same
- ❑ keep your price the same and make higher profits

For example, when sugar prices drop, a chocolate maker can choose to increase the size of his chocolates and earn the same profit, or leave the price as it is and earn more profit.

3.2 COMPETITION

The actions of competitors have a great influence on the price you set. You need to consider what competitors' reactions will be to your pricing decisions. This is not easy, but you must monitor both your competitors' price levels and their reactions to your pricing moves. For example, a competitor might respond to your actions by either cutting prices (price competition) or launching a new product (non-price competition). You can also use competitors' prices as a guide to where you can set your prices.

How can you collect information on your competitor's prices? There are a number of possible methods (Van der Walt *et al*, 1995: 420)

❑ checks by your sales force
❑ checks in stores where your products are stocked
❑ customer surveys

❑ marketing research such as focus group discussions (see chapter 2)
❑ buying competitors' products and estimating what their costs are

However you decide to do it, competitive price checks must become a periodic aspect of your research activities.

3.3 The type of product or service

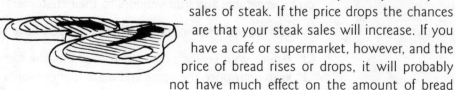

Price changes affect the sale of some products more than others. For example, if you open a butchery and the price of steak rises, it will probably affect your sales of steak. If the price drops the chances are that your steak sales will increase. If you have a café or supermarket, however, and the price of bread rises or drops, it will probably not have much effect on the amount of bread that you sell. To try to find out whether a price rise or fall will affect the sales of your product or service try to answer the following questions (Hutt & Stull, 1992:291):

❑ How much of the product or service do customers buy?
❑ Why do they buy?
❑ Is the product or service a luxury or a necessity?

The **customer profile** can help you to get some of these answers (see chapter 1).

3.4 Image

The **image** you decide on for your business is, to a large extent, affected by your price levels. If you want to have the image of a low cost supplier you will price low, keep expenses at a minimum and have a low cost location. On the other hand, if you want to have the image of quality you will price high, have good service support and a "good location".

3.5 Supply and demand

One of the most important factors affecting your price will be supply and demand. Hutt & Stull (1992:291) provide a useful definition of these terms.

> **Supply is the amount of a product or service that businesses provide at a given time and a given price.**
>
> **Demand is the amount of a product or service customers are willing and able to buy at a given time at a given price.**

When the demand for a product increases, the price of that product usually goes up. For example, let's assume you open up an exclusive wine shop stocking fine wines and liqueurs. When the KWV brandies win prizes at international competitions the demand for them rises, and so your price for them will also probably rise as the supply is fairly limited.

A change in supply also affects price, however. When the supply of Chardonnay wine from the wine estates and producers increases, the price of Chardonnay wine drops.

Always consider the effects of supply and demand in terms of new products, especially in the business analysis step of the new product development process discussed in chapter 4.

3.6 Environmental factors

Ennew (1993:177) provides a definition of environmental factors.

> **Environmental factors are those factors that affect the pricing decisions of all businesses and are outside the control of those businesses.**

Examples of environmental factors are government legislation, taxes and exchange rates. Think of the recent legislation that was passed concerning the requirements for minimum deposits on hire purchase agreements and the interest rates that are charged. Another good example of environmental factors are the changes over time to VAT. It is important for a small business person to be aware of these factors and their possible effects. This awareness can be achieved through contacts with your bankers, by reading business magazines and newspapers and by asking customers and suppliers.

Step 1 in setting prices: consider the factors affecting price.

Identify what type of factor each of the following represents? Answer by filling in the diagram.

EXAMPLE	TYPE OF FACTOR
❑ A fall in the Rand exchange rate	....
❑ Your product becoming very trendy	....
❑ Two new competitors entering the market with "specials"	....
❑ Choosing a new high income target market	....

4 OBJECTIVES OF PRICING

The second step in setting prices is to understand what you want to achieve through your pricing.

The aim or ultimate objective of pricing is to ensure that the small business **generates the sales needed to achieve its overall aims**. This requires you to identify three broad areas related to objectives (Ennew, 1993:173):

❑ increasing or maximising profits
❑ increasing market share
❑ increasing sales volume

In trying to increase or maximise profits the focus is on trying to make the most **profit** possible **in the long term.** This might be achieved by trying to obtain an average percentage of profit or trying to make the most profit you can on each sale. For example, a business may try to average 15% profit on every rand sold.

Some businesses focus on maintaining or increasing their market share. This means aiming to get **a bigger percentage of the business than your competitors**. The idea is to strengthen your position relative to that of the competitors (getting a bigger slice of the pie). For example, the objective might be to increase your share of the market from 20% to 30%.

Some businesses set their prices so as to maintain or increase the sales volume that they have achieved. The idea here is to **increase the overall sales figure.** An example of this objective would be to increase Rand sales from R600 000 per annum to R850 000 per annum. However, care needs to be taken. You can easily increase sales by decreasing your price, but you may not make any money doing so.

For many new businesses starting out the pricing objective may simply be to **survive** (Ennew 1993:173). Once the business is established the other types of objectives can become more viable. Survival is, in fact, the basic objective for any business.

> **Step 2 in setting prices: decide what are you trying to achieve.**

5 DECIDING ON WHAT YOUR BASIC PRICE LEVEL WILL BE

Once you have analysed the factors affecting price, and established what you want to achieve through pricing, you need to set the basic price level for your product or service.

> **In order to set a basic price, you need to consider three areas** (Kotler & Armstrong, 1994: 292):
>
> ❏ cost-oriented pricing
> ❏ customer-oriented pricing
> ❏ pricing relative to competition

5.1 Cost-oriented pricing

Many small businesses determine their basic price based on their costs. The idea is to set your price high enough to cover your costs and still make a profit (Van der Walt *et al*, 1995). Before we look at using costs as a basis for prices, we need to understand certain types of costs (Marx & Van der Walt, 1993:480).

TYPES OF COSTS	
FIXED COSTS	**VARIABLE COSTS**
salaries and wages equipment costs rentals	cost of materials cost of components

Fixed costs are those costs that stay the same irrespective of how many products are produced. Examples of these are salaries and wages, equipment costs or rental. All of these are incurred and stay the same whether the business is going full steam ahead or not making anything.

Variable costs are those costs that increase proportionately with the amount produced. Examples of these are costs of materials and components. The more products you make, the more raw materials are used up.

Let us look at three of the cost-oriented methods for setting a basic price, namely:

(a) Cost-plus pricing
(b) Rate of return pricing
(c) Breakeven analysis

(a) Cost plus pricing

Many small business people use this method. Here you determine the cost of the product and then add a set percentage to the cost for the profit margin. This method is easy to use and popular.

Assume you are a manufacturer of steel braais. After some financial analysis, you find the following:

Variable cost	R60
Fixed cost	R15 000
Expected sales	5 000 braais

The unit cost for each braai is:

$$\text{Unit cost} = \text{variable cost} + \frac{\text{fixed cost}}{\text{current sales}}$$

$$= \text{R60} + \frac{15\ 000}{5\ 000}$$

$$= \text{R63}$$

Assume you want a profit margin of 40% (also called the mark-up)

cost plus price $\quad = \dfrac{\text{unit cost}}{(1\text{-profit margin})}$

$$= \dfrac{R63}{\frac{40}{100}}$$

$$= R105$$

You will charge customers R105 for each braai and make a profit of R42 per unit R105-R63 = R42).

Using the cost-plus method, and using the information in the example above, calculate what the price will have to be:
(i)   to make a 50% mark-up
(ii) to make a 60% mark-up

(Answers will appear at the end of section 8)

(b) Rate of return pricing

This method is similar to the previous one but brings another aspect into the calculation, namely **the cost of investing your money into the business**. The idea is to set a price that gives you a certain rate of return on your total investment. This differs from the cost plus method, which gives you a certain profit margin per item sold.

To use this method you need four figures:
❏ an estimate of the units you will sell
❏ what each unit costs i.e. variable costs $+ \dfrac{\text{fixed cost}}{\text{estimated unit sales}}$
❏ the total amount of money invested in making and selling the product
❏ the target rate of return you want on your money

Assume you invested R30 000 to produce and sell steel braais. You want to make 30% return on your money, and you think you will be able to sell 5 000 braais. The variable cost is R60 per unit and the fixed costs are R15 000. The price you will set to achieve this rate of return is:

Target return price =
Unit cost + Target rate of return x total money invested estimated sales

$$= \dfrac{(60 \times 15\,000 +}{5\,000} \dfrac{(.30 \times 30\,000)}{5\,000}$$

$$= 63 + (.30 \times 6)$$

$$= 63 + 1.80$$

$$= R64\text{-}80$$

Using the information supplied in the example above, calculate what the price will have to be if you want:

(i)   a 35% rate of return
(ii)   a 40% rate of return

(Answers will appear at the end of section 8)

(c) Breakeven analysis

Breakeven analysis is really useful because it shows you how many units you will have to sell in order to cover your costs at a certain price. **At the breakeven point the money brought in (price x unit sales) exactly equals the total costs to make that many units**. Anything sold over that amount at that price means that the business makes money. Any sales in units less than that amount at that price means your business is losing money!

Assume you make and market braais. You want to price your braai at R70. Fixed costs are R15 000. Variable costs are R60 per unit.

Breakeven point in units $=$ $\dfrac{\text{Total fixed costs}}{\text{Selling price} - \text{variable cost per unit}}$

$=$ $\dfrac{\text{R15 000}}{\text{R70} - \text{R60}}$

$=$ 1 500 units

If your business sells 1500 units at R70 each it will cover all its costs. If it sells more than 1500 units at R70 each it will make a profit – R10 a unit.

Using the information supplied in the example above, calculate the breakeven point for:

(i)   a price of R80
(ii)   a price of R65

(Answers will appear at the end of section 8)

All of the cost-oriented approaches to determining your product's basic price have one common fault – they don't take into account that **the price can affect the amount of product that customers want**.

5.2 Customer-oriented pricing

In this approach pricing is not simply an issue of calculating a formula but, rather, **setting a price that is perceived by customers to be of value relative to what they get for the price**. Methods for customer-oriented pricing include (Van der Walt *et al*, 1995:490).

> backward pricing
> prestige pricing
> odd number pricing
> price lines
> skimming and penetration pricing
> bundle pricing

(a) Backward pricing

With this method you estimate the price that customers will be willing to pay for a product. You can find this out through market research, such as surveys or focus groups. This process will also help you to determine what the cost of making the product and cost of components should be, in order for you to be able to give the customers the product at the price they expect. Once you have this estimate you work backwards to see at what price you will sell to your distributors, so that **the price plus the distributors' margin equals the price customers expect to pay.**

(b) Prestige pricing

A business that follows this uses price to try to show the quality or prestige of its product or service. You set a high price, **assuming that customers think a high price means high quality.** This method is used often when your target market is the high income/high status type of customer. For example, you may start a carpet cleaning business and price yourself high because your target market is the upper income neighbourhood in your town.

(c) Odd-number pricing

This refers to the method of using prices ending in **odd numbers or under a round figure** (e.g. R4-99 instead of R5-00). Why would you do this? Two possible reasons are:

❑ Customers may think that R4-99 is much lower than R5-00 as it seems closer to R4-00 than R5-00.
❑ Many retail small businesses use odd-number pricing to force salespeople to ring up the sale on the cash register and give customers change.

(d) Price lines

This method is the use of **only a few prices for each of your product lines.** For example, you may use the price to indicate the levels of quality within your product line (e.g. economy line, value line, high quality line). One advantage of this approach is that your customer may have more choice. For example, you may open a store selling paint and stock three lines: an economy paint priced at R29-99 for 5 litres, a medium priced line at R49-99 for 5 litres and a high quality – high priced paint line at R69-99 for 5 litres.

Sometimes you may decide to price a line at a level that just covers costs in order to help the sales of other more profitable lines (Giles, 1994:89). This line is called a **loss leader**. The idea is to attract customers to the business with the loss leader, as they are likely to buy more expensive items as well. For example, a hardware store may price its white PVA paint low as a loss leader, hoping at the same time to get sales of its regular priced paint brushes, enamel paints and painting accessories.

(e) Skimming and penetration pricing

When introducing a new product to a market there are two different pricing options:

❑ skimming approach
❑ penetration approach

When you follow the **skimming approach** you price your product or service fairly high. You will follow this approach if:

❑ you don't have too many potential competitors
❑ customers don't know much about the product
❑ you don't need to recover your investment quickly

The aim of the skimming approach is to **maximise profits.**

A **penetration pricing approach** means that you price your product relatively low. You will follow this approach if:

❑ you have many potential competitors
❑ the customers do not easily accept high prices

The aim of penetration pricing is to penetrate or break into new markets, in other words, to **gain market share.**

Most of the time, the actual price chosen is between the two levels (the high level of skimming pricing and the low level of penetration pricing).

(f) Bundle pricing

In this approach you **combine two or more products or services in a single price.** For example, if you own a wine shop you might sell a bottle of red wine and a bottle of white wine at a set price for both. You might also sell a bottle of red wine with a wine glass and a copy of a wine guide for a set price. The idea is to provide the customer with a higher value product at a better price than if he/she were to buy each of the items individually. Many businesses introduce new products through bundle pricing and also use bundle pricing for special occasions such as Christmas. For example, you may be a leather goods manufacturer and offer a leather briefcase, wallet and leather notepad cover for a better price than if a customer were to buy each item individually.

What customer-oriented method for setting a price is being used in the following situations:

(a) You price a line so that costs are just covered in the hope that customers will buy more profitable lines.

....

(b) You price a product so that customers think they are paying a much lower price for the product/service.

....

(c) You price a product so that customers think the high price means high quality.

....

(d) You price a product to give customers a product/service at a price they will be willing to pay.

....

(e) You price a product to offer customers a pen, pencil and notepad at a better price than that of each of the items individually.

....

(f) You price a product that the customers know little about.

....

5.3 Pricing relative to competition

We have looked at using **costs** to determine your basic price. We have also looked at **customer-oriented pricing**. Another approach for setting your basic price level is to establish the level compared with competing products and service.

There are three options here (Hutt & Stull, 1992:293-294):

❏ **price above the market**
Pricing above the market means pricing your product or service higher than similar products or services sold by competitors. You need to justify the higher price in the customer's mind through better quality, higher image or better location.

❏ **price below the market**
Pricing below the market means pricing below similar products or services offered by competitors in order to make up for the lower profit through higher sales volume. The idea is to sell more than your competitors.

❏ **pricing at the market**
Pricing at the market means pricing to match your competitor's prices. You will take this approach if you don't have a substantial competitive edge to be able to price higher than competitors.

The trick with the basic price level is to price the product or service at the level that it **will sell,** not at the **level at which you want it to sell** (Pinson & Jinnett, 1993:81).

Step 3 in setting price: establish the basic price level.

⑥ DISCOUNTS

Once the basic price level is established the small business person needs to establish some flexibility in terms of that price. Giles (1994:89) provides a definition of discounts.

Discounts are reductions to the basic price.

The types of discounts which can be given include:

❏ **trade discounts**
  Trade discounts are given to retailers or wholesalers and are calculated on the retail price.

❏ **quantity discounts**
  Quantity discounts are offered to customers on the basis of the quantity that they buy. The idea is to motivate the customer to buy the larger amount.

❏ **cash discounts**
  Cash discounts are granted by the small business person to his/her customers if they settle their accounts within a certain period (usually 30 days).

❏ **seasonal discounts**
  Seasonal discounts are discounts offered in an effort to encourage the purchase of your product during special times of the year or day. For example, you may run a nursery and offer a seasonal discount on seeds just before planting season in spring.

❏ **geographical discounts**
  Geographical discounts are discounts based on how far away the customer is from the business. For example, you may offer to pay for railage to all your customers or reduce the cost for those customers who pick up their own purchases from you.

Step 4 in setting price: establish what discounts will apply

1. When (under what conditions) will you price your product or service at market level?

....

....

2. When will you grant

   (a) cash discounts? ....

   (b) quantity discounts? ....

7 PRICING FOR INDUSTRIAL MARKETS

We have already explained what an industrial product is (chapter 4). When you are dealing with an industrial product and thus an industrial market, you need to consider certain issues when setting a price (Adcock *et al*, 1993:208):

❑ **operating supplies**
Operating supplies are products such as envelopes, paperclips and the like. They are often packaged simply and sold in multiple packs, for example six boxes of paperclips per pack. This means that the price is usually low and quantity discounts are usually offered. Credit is also an issue to be considered here.

❑ **installations**
Installations are products which are installed, for example a baking oven installed for a pottery company. The price of this type of product is often negotiated, since it is usually specially made for the buyer's needs. It is important to establish the limits within which you will negotiate with the purchaser. For example, the minimum acceptable price for installing the baking oven might be set at R10 000 and the top price would depend on the purchaser's requirements.

❑ **raw material**
Raw materials are those included in or added to your products. For example, if you produce a range of chutneys and sauces the fruit purchased will be considered raw materials. It is important for customers seeking raw materials to get a trusted supply source and they may pay a price premium for it. Keep in mind that they will compare your price with that of your competitors, and may discuss this with suppliers during the year. Sometimes a contract is signed to supply at a certain price for a set period of time, with a quantity discount if customers buy more than an agreed upon amount.

☞

☐ **tenders**

Tenders refer to a situation where suppliers are asked to submit a price for a contract offered by a large customer, such as a city council, the defence force or the government. The customer specifies what is wanted and asks possible suppliers to put in a bid. For example, the defence force may ask a tender on video recorders for training. Here you will need to do very detailed costing analysis and also be aware of who the competition is. You then work out a price, based on both your knowledge of the competitors and how badly you want the business!

What are the possible price considerations for the following industrial products?

1 office desks ....

....

2 air conditioning maintenance service ....

....

....

3 city council tender for overalls ....

....

....

⓼ CREDIT

Many small businesses have to offer credit to their customers to stay competitive and to build their business. Longenecker *et al*, (1994:338) provide a useful definition of credit.

Credit is when the seller gives goods or services to the buyer in return for the buyer's promise to pay.

The main advantage of credit is that it allows you to **increase your sales** by bringing in new customers and allowing customers to buy more often. It allows you to promote to your credit customers and it also makes adjustments and exchanges of goods easier.

8.1 BENEFITS OF CREDIT

The use of credit offers benefits to both the buyer and the seller. For the buyer in a small business in particular, it can help you to operate your business better by allowing you some degree of financial breathing space.

The benefits for the small business that offers credit are that it can:
- ❏ create a closer relationship with your customer
- ❏ give you the chance to sell via the phone or mail
- ❏ allow your customers to buy whenever they want
- ❏ help you stay competitive compared with other suppliers

The benefits of credit to customers include:
- ❏ the facility of "buy now, pay later"
- ❏ better records of purchases
- ❏ easier adjustments and exchanges
- ❏ more convenience
- ❏ building a credit history

8.2 Kinds of credit

There are two broad categories of credit (Longenecker *et al*, 1993:339).

> **Consumer credit is credit offered to customers who purchase for personal or family use.**
>
> **Trade credit is granted to customers who are business firms.**

Let us consider the different types of credit for consumers or the trade.

Consumer credit usually comes in three forms:
- ❏ **open charge account**
  With an open charge account the customer gets the product when purchased and must pay when billed, usually by the end of the month. This is the usual business account.

- ❏ **instalment accounts**
  With an instalment account the customer must pay a deposit and pay the balance over a specified period of time. There is usually interest charged on the balance. This is the usual method for purchasing durable products such as washing machines and television sets. Note that this is subject to legislation and the small business person needs to be aware of the laws. The hire purchase agreement is an example of this type of credit.

❑ **revolving charge account**

With a revolving charge account the customer can buy from you at any time up to a certain limit. Interest is charged on the amount not settled at the end of the month. For example, if you are a vegetable trader you may allow a customer to purchase from you for up to R500-00 a month.

If you offer **trade credit** then most of the time you offer **a discount for paying early**. For example, if customers pay the invoice within 10 days, they may get a 2% discount off the invoice amount. If they don't pay within 10 days the full amount of the invoice becomes due within 30 days.

Keep in mind that a small business person can also negotiate to extend his/her own payment period. For example, you may negotiate with your suppliers to pay your account at 60 or 90 days, and this will allow you some financial breathing space.

8.3 Questions you need to ask

To evaluate any application for credit that you get you need to ask four questions (Longenecker *et al*, 1983:343):

❑ Can the buyer pay as promised?
❑ Will the buyer pay?
❑ If so, when will the buyer pay?
❑ If not, can he/she be forced to pay?

To grant credit you should be able to answer "yes" to the first, second and fourth questions and answer "on time" to the third question.

To check out possible credit customers you can use the services of **trade-credit agencies** or **credit bureaus,** which keep credit information on business firms or customers respectively. The idea is to reduce the risk of not being able to obtain the money that is owed to you, or at least to keep these bad debts to a minimum!

Step 5 in setting price: decide on the credit terms you will offer to customers.

ANSWERS TO ACTIVITIES

Activity 5.1.1	(a)	(i)	R126	(ii)	R157-50
Activity 5.1.2	(b)	(i)	R65-10	(ii)	R65-40
Activity 5.1.3	(c)	(i)	750 units	(ii)	3000 units

9 SELF-EVALUATION

9.1 Terms you have learned

Explain each of the following:

- ❑ price
- ❑ bartering
- ❑ supply
- ❑ demand
- ❑ environmental factors
- ❑ fixed costs
- ❑ variable costs
- ❑ loss leader
- ❑ discounts
- ❑ credit
- ❑ consumer credit
- ❑ trade credit

9.2 Quiz

Answer the following questions

(i)   What are the two roles that price plays in marketing?

1. ....   2. ....

....

....

(ii)   Compare the way a customer looks at price to the way a supplier looks at price

Customer	Supplier

(iii) Name some ways that you can get information on your competitor's prices:

1. ....

2. ....

3. ....

4. ....

5. ....

(iv) List the six factors that affect price:

1. ....

2. ....

3. ....

4. ....

5. ....

6. ....

(v) What are the three broad areas for pricing objectives?

1. ....

2. ....

3. ....

(vi) Assume that you have opened a small business making and supplying atchar in small bottles. After some financial analysis you know the following:

variable costs   =   R3-50

fixed costs   =   R15-000

expected sales   =   3 000 bottles

(a) If you wanted a 20% mark-up what will the price be if you follow cost-plus pricing?

(b) In the situation above, how much profit will you make per bottle?

(c) Assume you decide on a final price of R9-99 per bottle. How many bottles will you have to sell to break even?

(vii)   When will you follow skimming or penetration pricing strategies?

penetration strategy	skimming strategy
When used:	When used:

(viii) What are the three options when pricing relative to competitors?

1	2	3

(ix)   The basic price can be adjusted through the use of discounts. List five-possible discounts that you can offer and explain when to use each kind of discount?

Type of discount	When to use
1.	1.
2.	2.
3.	3.
4.	4.
5.	5.

(x)   The use of credit offers benefits both to the customer and to the small business. What are these benefits?

Benefits to suppliers	Benefits to customers
❏	❏
❏	❏
❏	❏
❏	❏
❏	❏

(xi)   Fill in the boxes with the five steps to follow in setting your price:

1.
2.
3.
4.
5.

9.3 Case study

THE MAIN ATTRACTION OF PEP STORES

"The main attraction of Pep Stores is price", says Basil Weyers, managing director of Pep Stores. "We sell consistently at low prices. We never have a sale. Our goods are offered every day at sale prices. We offer value for money." Pep Stores has a very low mark-up and is proud of its claim that it is the cheapest store in town.

Pep has a uniform pricing policy which ensures that an item will cost the same at any Pep store. Pep's policy is to sell quality products at a low price to the lower income group.

But just how does Pep succeed in offering continuously low prices? There are a number of contributing factors, some of which are included below:

- ❑ Volume bargaining power
- ❑ Lean management structure
- ❑ Simplified systems
- ❑ Tight cost controls
- ❑ Pep is a cash store which eliminates bad debts and lost interest on outstanding payments. To help the consumer lacking the necessary purchasing power, Pep has a lay-by system and also accepts credit cards.
- ❑ Pep owns some of its suppliers, making cost and quality control easier.
- ❑ The staff is small but very well trained, which makes staff members effective and productive.
- ❑ The outlets are small and relatively simple.
- ❑ Pep is saving by curbing stock losses.

Any competitor thinking of competing against Pep will have to consider the above achievements carefully.

Source: Adapted from Van der Walt, A. & Machado, R. (eds.). 1992. *New marketing success stories*. Southern: Johannesburg, p. 189.

1. How does Pep price itself relative to the competition?

2. What is the Pep policy towards credit?

3. What factors have affected the pricing followed by Pep?

4. What pricing objective do you think Pep has adopted?

10 REFERENCES

Adcock, D., Bradfield, R., Halborg, A. & Ross, C. 1993. *Marketing principles and practice*. Pitman: London.

Ennew, C.T. 1993. *The marketing blueprint*. Blackwell: Oxford.

Frain, J. 1994. *Introduction to marketing*. 3rd edition. Pitman: London.

Giles, G.B. 1994. *Marketing*. 6th edition. Pitman: London.

Hutt, R.W. & Stull, W.A. 1992. *Marketing: an introduction*. South Western: Cincinnati.

Kotler, P. & Armstrong, G. 1994. *Marketing: an introduction*. 3rd edition. Prentice-Hall: Englewood.

Longenecker, J.G., Moore, C.W. & Petty, J.W. 1994. *Small business management: an entrepreneurial emphasis*. South Western: Cincinnati.

Majaro, S. 1993. *The essence of marketing*. Prentice-Hall: London.

Marx, S. & Van der Walt, A. (eds.). 1993. *Marketing management*. 2nd edition. Juta: Cape Town.

Pinson, L. & Jinnett, J. 1993. *Target marketing for the small business*. Upstart: Dover.

Van der Walt, A. & Machado, R. (eds.). 1992. *New marketing success stories*. Southern: Johannesburg.

Van der Walt, A., Strydom, J.W., Marx, S. & Jooste, C.J. (eds.). 1995. *Marketing management*. 3rd edition. Juta: Cape Town.

DISTRIBUTION: GETTING YOUR PRODUCT TO THE CUSTOMER

6

1 LEARNING OBJECTIVES

After you have studied this chapter you should be able to:

- ❑ define what is meant by distribution
- ❑ identify the choices of distribution intensity
- ❑ distinguish between different types of middlemen
- ❑ describe the different types of distribution channels
- ❑ discuss the factors affecting the selection of a distribution channel
- ❑ pinpoint the causes of conflict in a channel
- ❑ evaluate different ways of controlling a distribution channel
- ❑ evaluate the location factors that need to be considered

2 INTRODUCTION

Distribution concerns finding the best outlet(s) for customers to receive the products or services that you offer, and keeping the outlets supplied so that those who want to buy are able to do so (Majaro, 1993:140). The fact is that at some point the small business will need a **distribution strategy,** to ensure that its products arrive safely at the right place at the right time, thus helping to ensure maximum customer satisfaction.

We can define distribution quite clearly.

> **Distribution is the establishment of a system that gets your product to where the customer wants to buy it.**

In order to do this you will have to decide on a **channel of distribution,** for which Hutt & Stull (1992:310) provide a useful definition.

> **A distribution channel is a system of people and organisations that get products or services from the producer to the customer.**

A simple way of looking at a distribution channel is as a pipeline, through which products flow from the producer to the customer. Within this pipeline are businesses that help in getting the product to the final customer. Examples of such businesses are wholesalers and retailers. These businesses are termed **middlemen** or **intermediaries**.

> **A middleman or intermediary is a business that helps move the product or service from the producer to the customer through the distribution channel.**

For example, a leather manufacturer may sell his leather goods to a leather goods wholesaler, who sells the product to retailers such as Pakwell's. Customers will be able to purchase the leather goods at Pakwell's. The leather wholesaler and Pakwell's can then be termed middlemen or intermediaries.

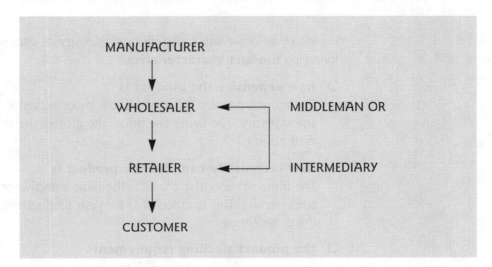

CHOOSING THE INTENSITY OF DISTRIBUTION

One of the first decisions for a small business person to make is on **how many potential outlets** will carry his product. This is called the **intensity** of distribution for the business. This intensity will depend on:

❑ **where the marketer is (location); and**
❑ **the characteristics of the product**

> **There are three choices available for the intensity of distribution**
> (Marx & Van der Walt, 1993:300-301):
>
> ❑ **intensive distribution**
>   With intensive distribution you try to make your product available at all possible outlets. This means you will use all possible middlemen. Branding is important here because you need to ensure that the stock moves well. Examples of products that follow this route are chocolate bars and cigarettes.
>
>   ☞

❑ **selective distribution**
With selective distribution you choose fewer outlets than intensive distribution but take care in choosing which to use. Shopping products, such as furniture and clothes, are examples of products which are suited to this type of intensity.

❑ **exclusive distribution**
With exclusive distribution, you purposely limit the number of people who carry your product. Examples of this are jewellery products. Franchises also follow this type of intensity. For example, a chocolate manufacturer may decide to supply only sweet (candy) stores in upmarket shopping centres in the big cities.

How do you know which distribution intensity to choose? It depends on the following **product characteristics**:

❑ **how expensive the product is**
The more expensive the product, the more exclusive or selective (limited) the intensity. The lower the price, the greater the tendency for intensive distribution.

❑ **how technically complex the product is**
The more complex the product, the more selective or exclusive should be the intensity. This is especially so if your product requires specialist training or knowledge.

❑ **the product's selling requirements**
If advice or sales assistance will be needed, you should tend towards selective or exclusive distribution. If the product is suitable for self-service outlets, consider intensive distribution.

❑ **the product's service requirements**
If there is a need for installing, maintaining or repairing the product, tend towards selective/exclusive distribution.

Step 1 in distribution: decide on intensity.

4 TYPES OF MIDDLEMEN

In talking about channels of distribution it is important to know the different types of middlemen that can be chosen. There are **three** different types (Marx & Van der Walt, 1993:269-277):

❑ sales middlemen
❑ wholesalers
❑ retailers

What are the differences between them? **Wholesalers and retailers are called resellers**.

> **A reseller is a middleman who actually owns the products he handles.**
>
> **A sales middleman brings producers and retailers into contact with one another but does not actually own the product being handled.**

A **sales middleman's** job is to be the link between the different people in the distribution channel.

4.1   Sales middlemen

The two most common examples of sales middlemen are **brokers** and **agents**.

A small business that has no salespeople usually uses agents to sell its products to wholesalers or retailers. **Agents help a small business gain sales and usually charge a commission for their services**. The agent usually gets a set percentage of the sales value as a fee for the service. For example, a manufacturer of women's dresses may use an agent to visit boutiques to sell his/her dresses to them.

A broker usually just brings buyers and sellers together. The idea is to make negotiations possible between buyers and sellers. The person who asked for the service is the one who pays the broker. Insurance broking and real estate broking are two common examples of a broker's activities.

4.2 Wholesalers

A business that **gets more than 50% of its sales income from selling to other businesses or organisations** is termed a wholesaler. Makro, for example, is a wholesaler. This does not mean that it does not sell to private customers at all, but that this piece of its business is less than half.

There are a number of different kinds of wholesalers:

❑ **cash and carry wholesalers**
The cash and carry wholesaler is where a shop owner goes, gets what he/she wants and pays cash for it. The shop owner has to transport his own goods.

❑ **rack-jobber**
The rack-jobber is a middleman who manages shelf space in retail stores. This kind of wholesaler usually specialises in certain areas (e.g. painting supplies) and ensures the shelves in the shops are stocked with the product. The shop owner then gets a set margin on the products that are sold.

❑ **truck-jobbers**
The truck-jobber is a middleman who goes from shop to shop, delivering perishable products (products that do not last long), such as vegetables and fruit.

❑ **mail order wholesalers**
The mail order wholesaler uses catalogues to inform customers of what is available and then sends out products that are ordered, usually on a cash-on-delivery (COD) basis.

4.3 Retailers

A business that sells **50% or more of its total sales to the general public for private or home use,** is termed a retailer.

There are many kinds of retailers:

❑ **general dealers**

General dealers have a very wide variety of products and are often found in rural areas.

❑ **department stores**

Department stores are large stores that have a fairly wide range of products in different departments, such as clothing, haberdashery, cosmetics, crockery and so on. Examples are Stuttafords and Garlicks.

❑ **speciality stores**

Speciality stores have only a few product lines but a great deal of variety in those lines. Examples of these are jewellery stores.

❑ **chain stores**

Chain stores are similar stores in various places that are controlled by one business. Examples of chain stores are Shoprite/Checkers, and Pick 'n Pay.

❑ **supermarkets**

Supermarkets are self-service stores offering a fairly wide variety of grocery and household products. Spar stores are a good example of supermarkets.

❑ **hypermarkets**
Hypermarkets are large stores with a wide product range, low prices, sizeable parking and a fairly large target market. Examples are the Pick 'n Pay Hypermarkets around the country.

❑ **spaza shops**
Spaza shops are small shops in the townships and informal areas that stock limited quantities of staples.

Step 2 in distribution: decide on types of middlemen you will need.

1. What sort of middleman (category) and specific type of middleman would you need for the following situations:

SITUATION	CATEGORY	SPECIFIC TYPE
a) You own a real estate business and pay somebody to make negotiations possible between buyers and sellers.	sales middleman	real estate broker
b) You own a hardware store and use the services of a paint supplier to keep your shelves stocked with painting supplies.	....	....

☞

114

SITUATION	CATEGORY	SPECIFIC TYPE
c) You manufacture tracksuits and pay someone a commission to sell your range to wholesalers, retailers and the public.	....	....
d) You are the owner of a café which also sells fruit and vegetables.	....	....

2. What two factors will influence your choice of the number of potential outlets that should distribute your product or service?
   a) ....
   b) ....

CHANNELS OF DISTRIBUTION

A distribution channel can be **direct** or **indirect**. Longenecker *et al* (1993:383) provide useful definitions.

> **A direct channel is a distribution channel where there is no middleman between the producer and the customer.**
>
> **An indirect channel is a distribution channel with one or more middleman between the producer and the final customer.**

A leather manufacturer who sells to customers from his factory is using a direct channel of distribution. If the manufacturer sells to leather goods stores, who then sell to customers, he/she is using an indirect channel. Of course, nothing stops the leather manufacturer from using both direct and indirect channels, and this is called a **multi-channel distribution strategy**.

DIRECT CHANNEL	INDIRECT CHANNEL
Leather manufacturer	Leather manufacturer
↓	↓
↓	↓
↓	Leather goods stores
↓	↓
↓	↓
Customers	Customers

Let us look at possible channels for consumer and industrial products.

5.1 Marketing channels for consumer products

We have already said that consumer products are for use by **individuals or families**. Examples of this type of product are cakes and household appliances. What channels might be used by a small business producing consumer goods? Some of the possible options are shown and discussed below (Hutt & Stull, 1992:311-313).

CONSUMER PRODUCTS: VARIOUS DISTRIBUTION CHANNELS				
PRODUCER	**PRODUCER**	**PRODUCER**	**PRODUCER**	**PRODUCER**
↓	↓	↓	↓	↓
↓	↓	↓	Agent	Agent
↓	↓	Wholesaler	↓	↓ Wholesaler
↓	↓	↓	↓	↓
↓	Retailer	Retailer	Retailer	Retailer
↓	↓	↓	↓	↓
Customer	Customer	Customer	Customer	Customer

❏ **producer to customer**
The producer to customer distribution channel is short because there is no middleman. The small business can use its own salesforce or mail catalogues. Examples of businesses that use this channel are Tupperware and the book clubs and CD clubs that sell through the mail. Most service businesses (for example, dry cleaners) use a direct channel such as this.

❏ **producer to retailer to customer**
The producer to retailer to customer distribution channel occurs where the small business uses a retailer, such as a supermarket or spaza shop, to sell to customers.

❏ **producer to wholesaler to retailer to customer**
The producer to wholesaler to retailer to customer distribution channel is used by many small businesses. For example, a manufacturer of paint brushes might sell to a hardware wholesaler who then sells to hardware stores all over the region.

❏ **producer to agent to retailer to consumer**
The producer to agent to retailer to consumer distribution channel is commonly used by many small businesses who cannot afford their own salesforce and who rely on agents to sell for them. For example, a clothing manufacturer might hire an agent to sell for him/her to all the independent clothing stores.

❑ **producer to agent to wholesaler to retailer to consumer**
The producer to agent to wholesaler to retailer to consumer distribution
channel is often used when many small businesses sell to a large number of
wholesalers around the country. For example, a hair product producer might
use agents to sell to wholesalers who then sell to retailers.

5.2 Marketing channels for industrial products

Industrial products, which are used in the **production of services or other
products**, generally follow four types of distribution channels (Hutt & Stull,
1992:313).

```
              INDUSTRIAL PRODUCTS
         COMMON DISTRIBUTION CHANNELS

   PRODUCER      PRODUCER      PRODUCER      PRODUCER

      ↓             ↓             ↓             ↓
      ↓           Agent           ↓           Agent
      ↓             ↓          Industrial   Industrial
      ↓             ↓          distributor  distributor
      ↓             ↓             ↓             ↓
      ↓             ↓             ↓             ↓
   Industrial    Industrial    Industrial    Industrial
     user          user          user          user
```

❑ **producer to industrial user**
Most industrial products are sold directly to the user. For example, an overall manufacturer might sell overalls direct to factories.

❑ **producer to agent to industrial user**
If a small business is not able to sell its own product it might use an agent
to do it. Agents are also useful when you are introducing a new product or
going into a new market because they can use their contacts and experi-
ence in the industry to get sales.

❑ **producer to industrial distributor to industrial user**
The industrial distributor acts like a wholesaler and usually handles products that are not highly priced, such as office equipment, office supplies
and operating supplies. Industrial distributors usually carry sizeable stock
to be able to deliver promptly to customers.

❑ **producer to agent to industrial distributor to user**
Here the small business person who cannot afford his/her own salesforce
can use an agent to reach the important distributors for the product.

The question of whether or not to use a direct channel requires careful consideration. You have to consider many factors and weigh up which channel option will be best for your business. A number of the factors to consider are shown below.

Factors which point to using a direct distribution channel **include:**

❑ a technical product that needs demonstration
❑ products that need supervised testing
❑ the need to go into long and complicated negotiations
❑ a product that needs specialised after-sales service
❑ lack of active selling by middlemen
❑ not being able to convince existing channels to carry stock
❑ very high middlemen profit margins
❑ very concentrated industrial markets – few buyers

Factors which point against using a direct distribution channel:

❑ lack of financial resources
❑ need to use resources elsewhere in a business
❑ lack of know-how in getting distribution
❑ not enough of a product mix to operate on your own
❑ a large number of potential buyers widely scattered

Source: Giles, G.B. 1994. *Marketing.* 6th edition. Pitman: London, pp. 173-174.

Step 3 in distribution: decide which channel or channels you will use for your marketing distribution.

What type of channel will the following use?

❑ general dealer...
❑ bakery business..
❑ garden bulb manufacturer ....
❑ insurance company ....
❑ library ....
❑ paint brush company ....

6   FACTORS AFFECTING THE SELECTION OF A DISTRIBUTION CHANNEL

As mentioned above, the main criterion in deciding on a distribution channel is how you will best be able to reach your customers. A number of factors will influence your choice of channels (Marx & Van der Walt, 1993:302-304).

Factors which influence the choice of distribution channels

- ❑ Customer characteristics
- ❑ Product characteristics
- ❑ Producer characteristics
- ❑ Competitor characteristics
- ❑ Environmental factors

6.1 Customer characteristics

Your choice of channel will depend on the needs and wants of customers. Once again, then, it is important that the small business person know his/her target market well. The **customer profile** can help in finding out how the customer purchases products and services.

You must consider **where the target market is located**. If it is quite spread out, you will need help to be able to reach it. If it is located in a fairly concentrated area (e.g. Gauteng), you may be able to go direct to the customer.

In terms of the target market, **customer preferences** are important. If customers buy small quantities but fairly often (e.g. sweets) you may need a longer distribution channel because you, yourself, will not be able to provide your product exactly as often as your customers want. If customers buy large quantities less often you may be able to handle distribution yourself.

The **number of potential customers** will also affect your choice of distribution channel. If there are many customers it may be difficult to deal with all of them directly.

The **type of customer** for your product will also affect the distribution channel you choose. If you aim your product at consumer markets the chances are you will use retailers. (Refer back to chapter three to review the characteristics of a target market and the customer profile.)

6.2 Product characteristics

Certain types of products need a fairly **short distribution channel.** These are:

- ❑ expensive products
- ❑ products that are bulky
- ❑ products that go out of fashion
- ❑ products that need specialised service
- ❑ products made especially to a customer's specification
- ❑ products that have a short shelf life (e.g. fresh milk)

Convenience type products, such as sweets and soap powder, usually have a **long** distribution channel because a single producer cannot make the product available to all the possible places that customers may go to purchase it.

6.3 Producer characteristics

The **internal resources** of a small business also influence the distribution channel length and, therefore, the choice of channel. Internal resources include the **business capital**, the **salespeople** and the small business owner's **managerial skills**. If the small business is strong in terms of internal resources, it will be less reliant on intermediaries. Conversely, if the small business owner does not have much **marketing knowledge** he will have to rely to some extent on intermediaries.

6.4 Competitor characteristics

The small business person needs to consider the channel which his/her competitors are using, and may then choose to use the same channel as the competition or choose to use another channel. As always, the small business person needs to consider the possible **reactions of the competitors** to his/her choice of channel (Ennew, 1993:217).

6.5 Environmental factors

The small business person will have to consider all the general factors in the **business environment**, such as the **economy**, **legislation** and **technology** (Adcock *et al*, 1993:220). The general state of the economy influences the choice of distribution channel. If the economy is tight, the channel should be short, as this is usually more economical. Legislation may affect your choice of channel: if, for example, you produce curios for export you will, by law, have to work through specific channels in order to qualify for export incentives. Technology too may influence your channel choice: for example, the advances in refrigeration technology that allow fresh produce or fish to be moved further afield.

All these factors above must be carefully considered when deciding **how long or short** your distribution channel will be.

Next you will have to **decide on a specific middleman.** A number of factors will influence your choice (Marx & Van der Walt, 1993:305).

Factors to consider when choosing a specific middleman
- ❑ Does the middleman reach your target market?
- ❑ Can he satisfy customer needs in terms of products and services?
- ❑ Does he have sufficient stock turnover so that stock does not sit on the shelf?
- ❑ Does he have the appropriate and correct storage facilities?
- ❑ Can he aggressively promote your product or service?
- ❑ Can he deal with competition?
- ❑ Will he work with you?
- ❑ How creditworthy is he?
- ❑ What are his managerial skills?

Step 4 in distribution: choose a specific middleman for your channel.

1. How will the location of your target market affect the location of your distribution channels?

    ....

    ....

2. Name two types of products that need a fairly short distribution channel.

    ....

    ....

3. How might the general state of the economy influence your choice of a distribution channel?

    ....

    ....

7 CONFLICT IN THE CHANNEL OF DISTRIBUTION

No matter how much care you take in choosing a channel of distribution, things don't always go according to plan. There is often conflict between members of a channel (e.g. retailers and wholesalers) or between the middlemen at a certain level (e.g. retailers).

There are many possible reasons for a middleman not co-operating with a small business person in the manner he/she would like (Marx & Van der Walt, 1993:307):

❑   the middleman sees himself as an **agent for his customers**, not his suppliers
❑   he may already **stock competitor's brands**
❑   yours may be a **totally new product** and he may not think it will sell well
❑   the **objectives** of the middleman and small business person may not be the same. For example, a cake manufacturer may want to make expensive cakes and the Tuisnywerheid he/she supplies may want cheaper cakes.
❑   unhappiness with the **price** of the product the middleman must pay
❑   **information** and **paperwork** required by the small business from the middleman
❑   unsatisfactory handling of **customer complaints**

The small business person will have to address all of these potential problems to ensure that he/she and the middleman make his/her product available to customers at the right place and time.

As a small business person you may face a further challenge: what if the middleman is not sure whether or not to stock your product? In this case the small business person needs to ensure that he/she convinces the middlemen of the **benefits** of stocking his product, including the **profits** he will make. To achieve this, you will need to prepare the following information:

❑ **advantages** of the product over competitors' products
❑ the **consumer needs** the product will satisfy
❑ the **market research** that has been done
❑ the **sales potential** of the product
❑ what will be done to help **promote** the product
❑ how the long term marketing plan will help the **middleman make profits**

> **Step 5 in distribution – decide how you will ensure co-operation in the channel.**

8 CONTROLLING THE CHANNEL

Once you have designed your channels of distribution and actually got them going you will need to work out how you will measure that they are performing: in other words, work out the **performance standards** by which you will judge the channels and the middleman.

> **A performance standard is the measure you will use to judge the effectiveness of the distribution channel and the middleman.**

There are many standards from which to choose:
❑ sales figures
❑ costs to you
❑ how promptly the middleman pays you
❑ complaints received from customers
❑ how much stock the middleman holds
❑ how often the middleman is out-of-stock
❑ shelf space and attention given to your products
❑ the middleman's sales effort
❑ customer attitudes to the middleman

Whatever standards you choose, you will use these standards to evaluate the performance of the channel. For example, a cake manufacturer may choose to evaluate the retailers he/she uses on the basis of sales per month, and speed of payment from the stores back to the manufacturer.

Step 6 in distribution: decide on the performance standards you will use to control your channels.

Explain how you will convince a middleman to sell a totally new educational toy you have just developed. The middleman thinks your product may not sell well.

....

....

....

9 LOCATING YOUR BUSINESS

The choice of location is one of the most important decisions influencing the success of a new small business. You must study and understand your customers to be able to choose a location that will meet their needs. The work you do in researching and analysing will pay dividends in choosing a good location. It is important to get location correct, because it is difficult and expensive to move again once you have established your business. The location decision is more important to some businesses than others. For example, the site chosen for a ladies' clothing boutique can make or break it, while the site for a painting contractor is not so important.

According to Longenecker *et al* (1994:219-222) **there are four aspects to consider when choosing a location:**
- ❏ personal preferences
- ❏ environmental conditions
- ❏ resource availability
- ❏ customer accessibility

9.1 Personal preference

Many small business owners prefer locating their business in their **home community** because of their familiarity with their own neighbourhood. It is also sometimes easier to establish credit where you are well known. You may also know potential customers better since they come from the same area – often friends and relatives are the small business person's first customers.

Many small businesses start out in a person's home, garage, or spare room. This saves that person the cost of renting space. Once the business gets established the business person can consider whether or not it is necessary to move out. An important aspect of achieving success in this situation is **separating the business and the home,** so that you give a professional image and can deal with customers without interference.

Another important consideration for the small business person thinking of starting a business from home is **zoning ordinances**, which are defined by Longenecker *et al* (1984:228).

> **Zoning ordinances are local laws regulating land use.**

The small business person must be aware of the zoning ordinances that will apply to him/her using his/her home.

A further option is the **"business hive"** type of facility provided by organisations like the Small Business Development Corporation.

> **A business hive is a facility that provides shared space, services and management advice to new small businesses.**

Hives are usually located in areas where there is some demand for the types of business found in the hive, and the small business person gets help and advice from those running the hive.

9.2 Environmental conditions

The small business person needs to consider carefully the general environment of the location, including factors such as **economics**, **competition**, **laws** and **community attitudes**. For example, if your business is a ladies' clothing boutique you need to choose a fairly upmarket location, preferably close to other boutiques so that customers can compare what is on offer.

9.3 Resource availability

Analysis of the resources available to the proposed location is important, as this will have a bearing on the business's chances of operating effectively.

Factors to consider in relation to resource availability:

❑ Is there land available?
❑ Is there a water supply?
❑ Is there electricity?
❑ Is there a labour supply?

❑ Are there transportation facilities?
❑ Is there a waste removal service?
❑ Are there raw materials available?

The availability of resources is especially important if your business will manufacture products, because specifically the availability of raw materials and a reliable supply of labour will be critical to your success.

9.4 Customer accessibility

If you are operating or starting a retail outlet or a service business you need to locate it where it is easy for your customers to get to you. For example, a tobacconist's shop or a hair salon requires a location with ease of access for customers, such as a small neighbourhood shopping centre or a large shopping centre like Sandton City.

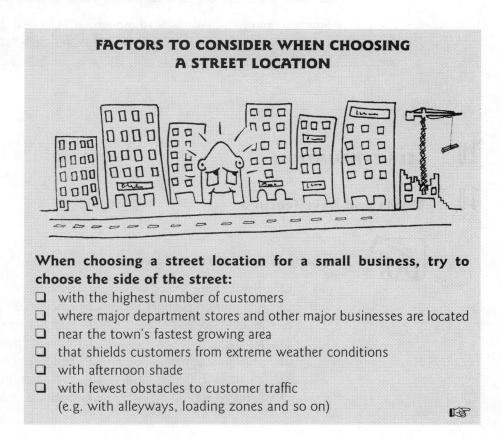

FACTORS TO CONSIDER WHEN CHOOSING A STREET LOCATION

When choosing a street location for a small business, try to choose the side of the street:
❑ with the highest number of customers
❑ where major department stores and other major businesses are located
❑ near the town's fastest growing area
❑ that shields customers from extreme weather conditions
❑ with afternoon shade
❑ with fewest obstacles to customer traffic
    (e.g. with alleyways, loading zones and so on)

Where not to locate your small business:

❏ areas with many abandoned or vacant buildings – it makes it look like you are in a dying area
❏ sites that are difficult or even impossible to reach (e.g. alleyways, narrow back streets)
❏ locations where many previous businesses have failed
❏ sites that suffer from heavy vehicle traffic
❏ sites that are poorly lit
❏ sites close to businesses that have long parking times (e.g. movie theatres)
❏ locations surrounded by businesses that do not complement your business (e.g. an upmarket men's clothing store in a shopping centre with factory shops)
❏ sites that have not been carefully studied or analysed

Source: Zimmerer, T.W. & Scarborough, N.M. 1994. *Essentials of small business management.* Macmillan: New York, pp. 369-370).

10 SELF-EVALUATION

10.1 Terms you have learned

Explain each of the following:

❏ distribution
❏ distribution channel
❏ middleman
❏ reseller
❏ sales middleman
❏ broker
❏ agent

❏ retailer
❏ wholesaler
❏ direct channel
❏ indirect channel
❏ performance standard
❏ zoning ordinance
❏ business hive

10.2 Quiz

Answer the following questions

(i)   With what is distribution concerned?

....

....

(ii) What do middlemen do that is so important?

....

....

(iii) What are the three options for intensity of distribution? Explain each one briefly.

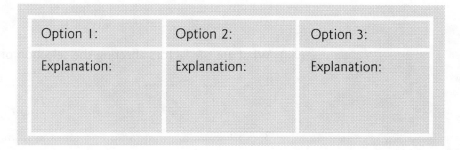

Option 1:	Option 2:	Option 3:
Explanation:	Explanation:	Explanation:

(iv) Identify four characteristics of the product that help determine what intensity to choose:

1. ....

2. ....

3. ....

4. ....

(v)   For each of the different types of middlemen below list some examples:

Sales middlemen	Wholesalers	Retailers
1.	1.	1.
2.	2.	2.
	3.	3.
	4.	4.
		5.
		6.
		7.

(vi) What is the difference between a direct and an indirect channel?

....

....

(vii) List the possible channels for marketing consumer and industrial products.

Consumer products	Industrial product
Possible channels:	**Possible channels:**
1.	1.
2.	2.
3.	3.
4.	4.

(viii) What are the factors affecting the selection of a distribution channel?

1. ....

2. ....

3. ....

4. ....

5. ....

(ix) Why is there often conflict in the distribution channel between the producer and the middleman?

....

....

....

....

....

....

(x) You are going to try to convince a prospective middleman to stock your product. He has never seen you or your product before. Identify six items that you will include in your presentation to him in order to convince him to stock your product:

1. ....

2. ....

3. ....

4. ....

5. ....

6. ....

(xi) You have a friend who wants to open a new butchery. He asks for your advice as to where he should locate his business. What four aspects of location should he consider?

1. ....

2. ....

3. ....

4. ....

10.3 Case study

EASY WAVES

Easy Waves, a company producing black hair care products, initially introduced its products in the key townships of the Gauteng area. Due to budgeting constraints, it was decided to concentrate first on Soweto and the East Gauteng townships. Consumers in these areas were also regular shoppers in the chain stores such as OK Bazaars.

The distribution of Easy Waves presented many challenges. At first the sales function for Easy Waves was handled by agents, who also worked for other businesses selling their products. The listing of Easy Waves with the major chains in both the wholesale and retail sectors proved to be difficult, yet management recognised it as an essential requirement for long term success. Acceptance of Easy Waves for sale in the key chain stores was achieved only after numerous presentations. Some of the problems that needed to be overcome were:

❏ buyers apparently preferred dealing with larger established companies or multinationals, rather than supporting smaller, innovative companies

❏ extremely large discounts and incentives were required to gain listings and this, of course squeezed the profit margins of Easy Waves

❏ agents did not give priority to Easy Waves products, which resulted in inadequate stock levels and low shelf-space shares.

The eventual successful trade acceptance of Easy Waves was due largely, in the opinion of Easy Waves management, to push and pull forces. Examples of push forces included promotional discounts to the trade while pull forces included sophisticated marketing techniques such as superior packaging and impactful advertising campaigns. The background of the Easy Waves management in both toiletries and marketing, along with its persistence and commitment, helped to break down trade resistance.

Once the listing with the major chain stores had been achieved and maintained, the focus shifted to distribution in the Transvaal, OFS/Lesotho, Natal, and Transkei/Ciskei. In order to gain quick distribution in these areas incentives were offered to agents, over and above normal agency commission rates, for reaching agreed upon sales and distribution targets. To help achieve this and to generate co-operation from the trade a number of sales promotion techniques were used:

❑ co-operative advertising
❑ in store promotional displays
❑ free-stock deals and promotional money
❑ demonstrations in the stores

Source: Van der Walt, A. & Machado, R. (eds.). 1992. *New marketing success stories*. Southern: Johannesburg, p. 87.

1. Where did Easy Waves first try to get distribution?
2. With what types of middlemen did Easy Waves deal?
3. Why was there resistance from the middlemen to Easy Waves?
4. Give examples of the actions of Easy Waves to successfully gain distribution.
5. What promotional techniques did Easy Waves use to get quick distribution in the rural areas?

11 REFERENCES

Adcock, D., Bradfield, R., Halborg, A. & Ross, C. 1993. *Marketing principles and practice*. Pitman: London.

Ennew, C.T. 1993. *The marketing blueprint*. Blackwell: Oxford.

Giles, G.B. 1994. *Marketing*. 6th edition. Pitman: London.

Hutt, R.W. & Stull, W.A. 1992. *Marketing: an introduction*. 2nd edition. South Western: Cincinnnati.

Longenecker, J.G., Moore, C.W. & Petty, J.W. 1994. *Small business management: an entrepreneurial emphasis*. South Western: Cincinnati.

Majaro, S. 1993. *The essence of marketing*. Prentice-Hall: London.

Marx, S. & Van der Walt, A. (eds.). 1993. *Marketing management*. 2nd edition. Juta: Cape Town.

Van der Walt, A. & Machado, R. (eds.). 1992. *New marketing success stories*. Southern: Johannesburg.

Zimmerer, T.W. & Scarborough, N.M. 1994. *Essentials of small business management*. Macmillan: New York.

7 PROMOTION: COMMUNICATING WITH YOUR MARKET

1 LEARNING OBJECTIVES

After you have studied this chapter you should be able to:

- ❏ identify the factors to consider in determining a promotional mix
- ❏ describe what promotion can achieve
- ❏ explain the seven steps in designing a promotional mix
- ❏ list the different ways of setting a promotional budget
- ❏ explain the advantages/disadvantages of the following promotion techniques:
  - advertising
  - sales promotion
  - publicity
  - personal selling

2 INTRODUCTION

Promotion is important because no matter how good your product or business is, you cannot be successful unless people **know** about it.

Ennew (1993:184) provides a good definition:

> **Promotion is the range of methods used by the small business to communicate with customers, employees and any other interested group.**

Let us examine this definition more closely. First, the small business can communicate with both current and potential customers. Second, communicating with employees is important because everyone in the business has to know what is going on. Third, always remember that promotion, important though it is, works together with the other three elements of the marketing mix (product, price, distribution). To be effective in your marketing, all aspects of the marketing mix need attention.

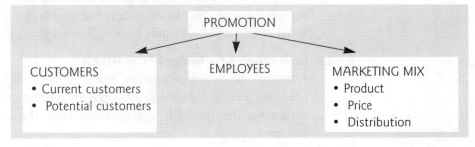

PROMOTION

CUSTOMERS
- Current customers
- Potential customers

EMPLOYEES

MARKETING MIX
- Product
- Price
- Distribution

In terms of promotion a small business has a large number of methods from which to choose. This choice of methods is called the **promotion mix** (Longenecker *et al*, 1991:359).

> **A promotion mix is the blend of promotion methods used by the small business to communicate.**

The main methods used to communicate are:

❑ advertising
❑ sales promotion
❑ publicity
❑ personal selling

We will discuss each of these methods later.

The choice of what promotion methods to use depends on a number of factors.

FACTORS TO CONSIDER IN DECIDING ON A PROMOTION MIX

There are four main factors to consider in relation to communicating with customers (Longenecker *et al*, 1994:359):

❑ **how widely the customers are scattered**
If customers are widely scattered, you will have to think of advertising; if not then a choice such as personal selling might be right. For example, a small business selling cakes will have to use promotion to let all its possible customers know what products and services it offers. However, if its customers are spread out all over the region, personal selling may be too expensive and time consuming and the small business might have to rely on advertising to communicate with customers.

❑ **the characteristics of the target market**
The customer profile which we discussed in earlier chapters will give you information as to how to reach your customers.

❑ **the type of product**
Certain products, by their nature, suggest certain methods of marketing rather than others. For example, a mass produced, low-tech, low priced product will be suited to advertising. By contrast, a product which has a high price and is fairly high-tech will need you to consider personal selling. Further if the product has significant service and maintenance aspects personal selling will be a viable option (Frain, 1994:245).

❑ **how much of a budget is available**
Although expensive promotion does not necessarily mean good promotion, the amount of money available for promotion will to a large extent determine the methods and options that the small business person will have.

All these factors need to be considered to determine what choices of promotion method the business person has.

> **Step 1 in communication: consider the factors determining how to communicate with customers.**

4   OBJECTIVES OF PROMOTION

Most small business people would say that the objective of promotion is to increase sales (Ennew, 1993:189). Although this is the end result that you hope to achieve, it is important to keep in mind that promotion deals with communication and you should think of **setting a communication objective**. Any promotion campaign has to start by setting a clear statement of what it is that you are trying to achieve. Adcock *et al* (1993:240) point out that through promotion you can:

❑   **inform**

Give information about a product, tell that it exists, say what it does, say where it can be obtained and so on. For example, a dry-cleaning store that has just opened may want to make the people in the area aware of its presence.

❑   **persuade**

Try to build up a good customer attitude to your business, tell why customers should use you over the competition, convince customers to try your business or to buy now. For example, a motor repair business might say that customers who own BMW cars should try it because the owners have been trained in BMW maintenance and have worked with BMWs for over twenty years.

133

❑ **remind**

Try to reassure customers who have already bought, increase the loyalty of those who have bought before, making sure you have established the groundwork for possible future sales. For example, a butchery may remind its customers that it has won the prize for the best boerewors in town.

Step 2 in communicating: decide what it is you are trying to do with your marketing communication to help you set communication objectives.

As a small business person you need to consider possible promotional objectives that may be of help in deciding what *your* promotional objectives will be.

EXAMPLES OF PROMOTION OBJECTIVES:

1 **Inform**
   - ❑ tell the market about a new product/service
   - ❑ suggest a new use for your product/service
   - ❑ tell customers about a price change
   - ❑ explain how the product/service works
   - ❑ describe available services
   - ❑ correct wrong impressions about your business
   - ❑ build up a good image

2 **Persuade**
   - ❑ build up a preference for your brand
   - ❑ try to get customers to switch to your brand
   - ❑ get customers to buy now
   - ❑ get customers to let you call on them to sell
   - ❑ change how customers think of your product/service

3 **Remind**
   - ❑ remind customers that they may need your product/service
   - ❑ remind customers where they can buy your product/service
   - ❑ remind customers about your product/service during off-seasons
   - ❑ keep customers aware of your product/service

Decide whether each of the following is trying to inform, persuade or remind. Tick your answer in the appropriate box.

	INFORM	PERSUADE	REMIND
❏ new, improved catering service			
❏ just opened – ladies' boutique			
❏ still the best boerewors in town			
❏ compare and decide – you will love our cakes			
❏ easy to use – cleans and shines all floors			
❏ just minutes away – call us for free delivery			
❏ winter is coming soon – have you had your car checked?			

5 DECIDE ON THE TARGET AUDIENCE

Once you know what it is that you want to achieve, you have to decide with whom you are going to communicate. These groups are called the **target audience.** Ennew (1993:189) provides a definition of the target audience.

The target audiences are the groups to whom you want to communicate your message.

The **target market** would probably make up a **target audience**, but there could be other groups involved. For example, if you have just opened up a motor repair business and have chosen the drivers of vehicles in your immediate neighbourhood as your target market, then your target audiences might be the small business owners in the area, the housewives in the homes around you and the drivers of automobiles. Note that you should treat each target audience separately, because their needs and information requirements are different. For example, the small business owners will be concerned with having their vehicles available for business, the housewives might be concerned with safety and reliability, and the automobile drivers in the area might be concerned with convenience.

It is important to find out what each target audience already knows about the business or product, so that you can work out what to do with your promotional effort. For example, it's no use telling the target audiences in the example above that you are better than the franchised automobile dealers for servicing cars if the target audiences don't even know that your business exists!

Step 3 in communicating: determine who the target audiences are and what they already know about your business.

Decide who the possible target audiences could be for the following:
- ❏ a small business designing and sewing matric dance dresses
- ❏ a gardening and irrigation service
- ❏ a small business making cakes and pies
- ❏ a small business removing household rubbish

DECIDE WHAT TO TELL THE TARGET AUDIENCE

Once you know who the target audiences are you will have to decide on your message, or what you want to tell them. This message will help you achieve your objectives. Your **knowledge of your customer** will be invaluable here because it is important that you get and hold their attention and so influence them. Your customer profile, information obtained from research and continuous contact with customers will help you to decide what to say to customers. **It is critical to remember that you must decide on your message based on your target audience.**

According to Ennew (1993:190) there are two aspects of any message:

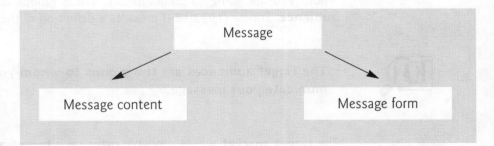

The message content is the basic idea and information that you want to get through to the target audience.

The message form is the combination of verbal, visual and audio signals that presents the message content to the target audience in the most suitable way.

The **content** of the message is important because you have to show:
- ❏ why your product is **different**
- ❏ the **benefits** that you offer to the customer
- ❏ why the customer **should buy your product** rather than the competitor's.

The **form** of the message also needs careful attention because it should **attract attention** and **maintain interest** long enough to get the message across.

You need to be especially careful to avoid being ambiguous or confusing to the target audience. It is in this area of marketing that marketing consultants or advertising agencies are especially helpful.

If you are unsure of the message that you want to put across you can always do research with your target audience to see if your message is clear, understandable and impactful. This kind of research will help you in fine tuning your message to be more effective (Giles, 1994:120).

Step 4 in communicating: decide what your message is going to be and how you will get it across to your target market.

7 DRAW UP A BUDGET

It is important to note that it has never been proven that sales volume depends on how much money you spend on promotion (Frain, 1994:247). This means that merely guessing as to how much to spend is not a good method of setting a promotion budget.

A promotion budget is the amount of money established for all your promotion activities.

There is no ideal method of setting a budget, but there are a number of different ways of setting a budget (Ennew, 1993:191-193):

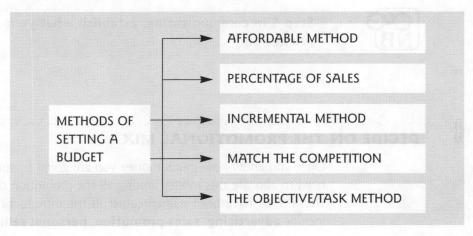

METHODS OF SETTING A BUDGET
- AFFORDABLE METHOD
- PERCENTAGE OF SALES
- INCREMENTAL METHOD
- MATCH THE COMPETITION
- THE OBJECTIVE/TASK METHOD

❑ **the affordable method**

Using the affordable method you determine the budget according to what you have available or what you can afford. A number of small businesses use this method because of their limited resources. For example, a business person opening a shoe repair business may decide that the business can only afford R3 000.00 for promotion spending in the first six months of the business.

❑ **percentage of sales**

With the percentage of sales method you decide that your promotion budget will be a certain percentage (e.g. 3%) of your sales. This could present a problem because it means, of course, that before you can promote you will need to have some sales. It is not a very good method to use when launching a new product or establishing a new business, or when business is generally bad.

❑ **incremental method**

Using the incremental method you base your budget on what was spent in a previous time period. For example, you add 5% to the promotion budget of the previous year. The problem here is that it is not related at all to your specific objectives.

❑ **match the competition**

With the 'match the competition' method you simply match the budget of the competitor. This means finding out what the competition spends. It also means ignoring the possible differences between you and your competitors. This method is not feasible for a totally new product (Anderson & Dobson, 1994:179).

❑ **the objective/task method**

Using the objective/task method you first determine what objective or task you want to achieve. Then you establish the tasks needed in your promotion to achieve this. Finally, you determine what that will cost – and that is your budget.

Which method is the most popular? For a small business person the simpler methods are often used, such as the affordable method, the percentage of sales method and the incremental method.

Step 5 in communicating: establish what your budget will be for promotion.

DECIDE ON THE PROMOTIONAL MIX

Once you know how much money you are going to spend on promotion you need to allocate this money among all the promotion tools that are available. These tools have been named earlier in the introduction to this chapter and include **advertising**, **sales promotion**, **personal selling** and **publicity**. The combination of these tools is called the promotion mix (Ennew, 1993: 192-193).

The promotion mix is the combination of promotion tools used by the small business person.

It should be clear that if you have a business dealing with industrial products you will probably emphasize personal selling, while if you have a consumer-product oriented company you will probably emphasize advertising and sales promotion. Each of the major promotion tools will be covered later in the chapter. The trick is to choose the promotion mix that will be the most cost effective for your specific products and customers (Ennew, 1993:193).

Step 6 in communicating: decide on what the promotion mix will be.

9 IMPLEMENT AND MEASURE RESULTS

The last step has two aspects to it. First, you must set up a **schedule of all the activities** needed to implement your promotion plan. Make sure you identify exactly who does what and establish the time by which these tasks must be completed. Without this schedule you will find it difficult to find the time to do all the things needed for an effective promotion effort. You cannot be effective without good planning.

Second, you need to ensure that you **evaluate all your promotion activities**. You need to be able to assess whether or not the promotions worked. You can only do this if you are clear as to what you were trying to achieve and exactly what it is you will measure. For example, if you decide your objective is to increase your target market's awareness of your store then you will measure what percentage of the target market knew you were around both before and after your promotion activities (e.g. an increase in awareness of your business from 10% to 60% in one year). It should be clear that you need to take care in deciding what your promotion objectives are.

10 ADVERTISING

Many small business people believe that advertising is not applicable to them because it is so expensive. Although advertising can be expensive it must be seen as an investment in the business. In fact, advertising is common among local small businesses, and is not only for large, national companies (Zimmerer & Scarborough, 1994:326). Think of the many advertisements (including classified advertisements) in the local newspapers. Think too of the radio ads for small business. The correct use of advertising should be a regular aspect of any successful and growing small business.

Longenecker *et al* (1994:367) provide a good definition of advertising.

Advertising is the impersonal presentation of a business idea through mass media.

According to Longenecker *et al* (1994:369) there are two basic types of advertising:

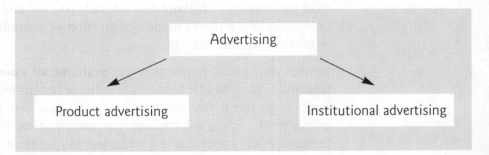

Product advertising is designed to make potential customers aware of a product or service and their need for it.

Institutional advertising is intended to raise customer awareness of a business.

For example, if you own a shoe repair business and you advertise a new, quick heel-repair service this is an example of product advertising. If you advertise the shoe repair business itself this is an example of institutional advertising.

PRODUCT ADVERTISING	INSTITUTIONAL ADVERTISING
QUICK HEAL! HEEL REPAIR.	SHOE REPAIRS.
Advertisement ↓ new quick heel-repair	Advertisement ↓ business itself

Whatever type of advertising you decide to use, it is no use simply advertising once. If you decide to use advertising it is important to use it regularly. The problem, however, is deciding where to advertise. The type of business you are advertising is an important consideration here.

If you open up a real estate agency you will probably use the home supplement of your local newspaper and the Yellow Pages. A plumbing business will also use the Yellow Pages and advertise on the sides of the business's vehicles as well.

Below is a summary of the advantages and disadvantages of the various possible places to advertise (Zimmerer & Scarborough, 1994:328-345).

10.1 Newspapers

Most small businesses use local newspapers to get their message to their target market.

The **advantages** of newspapers are that:
- ❏ they cover a specific geographical area, so you don't waste money on areas that may not be important to you
- ❏ they are fairly flexible in terms of where the advertisement is placed in the newspaper
- ❏ they offer help in designing the advertisement
- ❏ the costs are relatively low compared to other alternatives

The **disadvantages** of newspapers are that:
- ❏ you may still get some newspaper readers who are not in your target market
- ❏ the quality of reproduction in newspapers is often not very good
- ❏ the location of the advertisement may not be the best or most prominent
- ❏ the life of the advertisement tends to be short (newspapers are rarely kept for long)
- ❏ many South Africans are illiterate or only semi-literate or do not buy newspapers

10.2 RADIO

Care as to exactly what time, stations and programme that you choose for your radio advertisement (or ad) ensure that you are able to reach your target market fairly effectively. Radio is used by many retailers, in particular, and has its own **advantages**:

❑ almost all South Africans either own or have access to a radio

❑ radio stations have fairly well defined target markets of their own and a good fit may exist with your own target market

❑ radio ads are fairly cost effective to produce and can be changed fairly easily

❑ radio is a bit more persuasive than newspapers since it uses sound to try to influence customers

There are some serious **disadvantages**, however, associated with the use of radio:

❑ there is no guarantee that your target audience will actually hear your advertisement

❑ you need to repeat the ads for them to be effective

❑ the message in the advertisement has to be brief

A number of developments have made the use of radio a viable option for small business advertising. Many local radio stations (such as Radio Highveld and Jakaranda) now offer special packages to small businesses. Small business owners need to make themselves aware of all the special offers available by contacting their local radio stations and asking for information in this regard.

Many stations also offer combinations of radio and magazine/newspaper advertising. A radio listener is made aware of a product/service and is referred to a specific magazine or newspaper for further details. The small business owner may be able to negotiate a better deal through this method.

Another creative option for the small business to maximise its exposure is to offer the radio stations a talk, or a series of talks, on specific topics. For example, a nursery may offer a series on indigenous gardening and place advertising on the station before and after the talks. If you do something like this always be sure to mention your telephone number for those potential customers who may want to contact you. The point to emphasise here is that the small business person must be innovative in his/her approach to media so as to be able to get the most out of the budget.

GUIDELINES FOR EFFECTIVE RADIO ADS

❑ **Mention the business often**: This is the single most important and inflexible rule in radio advertising. Also make sure listeners know your location. If the address is complicated, use landmarks.

❑ **Stress benefit to the listener**: Don't say "Bryson's has new autumn fashions" — say "Bryson's autumn fashions make you look stylish and chic."

❑ **Use attention getters:** Radio has a whole battery — music, sound effects, unusual voices. Crack the barrier with sound. ☞

❑ **Zero in on your audience**: Know to whom you're selling. Radio's selectivity attracts the right audience. It's up to you to communicate in the right language.

❑ **Keep the copy simple and to the point**: Don't try to impress listeners with complicated vocabulary. After all "to be or not to be" may be one of the best-known phrases in the English language ... and its longest word has only three letters.

❑ **Write for the ear**: Write conversationally.

❑ **Prepare your advertising copy or script**: Underline words for emphasis.

❑ **Triple space**: Type cleanly. Make the voice artist rehearse.

❑ **Use positive, action words**: Use words like "now" and "today", particularly when you're writing copy for a sale. Radio has qualities of urgency and immediacy. Take advantage of them by including a time limit or the date a sale ends.

❑ **Put the listener in the picture**: Radio's theatre of the mind means you don't have to talk about a new car. With sounds and music you put the listener behind the wheel.

❑ **Sell early and often**: Don't wait till the end to give the selling message. You don't have too many seconds. Use them all to your benefit. Don't be subtle.

❑ **Focus the radio spot on getting a response**. Make it clear what you want the listener to do. Don't try to get a mail response. Use phone numbers only, and repeat the number three times. End the spot with the phone number.

❑ **Don't stay with a loser**. Direct response ads produce results right away – or not at all. Don't stick with a spot that's not generating sales. Change it!

Source: Adapted from Zimmerer & Scarborough, 1994:332.

10.3 Magazine

There are many general interest magazines aimed at consumers (e.g. *Huisgenoot/You, Bona, Fair Lady*) and trade magazines aimed at specific types of businesses (e.g. *Professional Caterer*). There are also special interest magazines aimed at people with particular interests (e.g. *Getaway, SA Home & Garden*, and *Wine*).

There are many **advantages** to using magazines:

❑ readers tend to keep them for a long time and they often get read and passed along by more than one person
❑ the customers who buy special interest magazines tend to have a high degree of interest in specific products or services that may line up with what you offer
❑ the quality of the advertisements is usually very good

The main **disadvantages** of using magazines are that:

❑ they tend to be costly, both in terms of space in the magazine and making the advertisement
❑ magazines have long lead times for booking advertisements
❑ it is very important to get a prominent position in the magazine, otherwise the advertisement may not be noticed

10.4 Outdoor ads

A number of small businesses and retailers are using outdoor ads or billboards to advertise, especially in rural areas. For the small business there are a number of **advantages** to using outdoor ads:

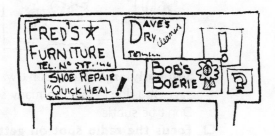

❑ they reach a large number of potential customers
❑ they can be designed to match a message to the target audience
❑ they are fairly cost effective
❑ they allow small business people to take advantage, with their suppliers, of cooperative advertisements. This means that a retailer and a supplier might share the costs of putting up a billboard.

There are also some **disadvantages** of outdoor ads:

❑ often the audience is exposed to the billboard for only a short period of time – so the message itself must be short
❑ there are environmental considerations and legal restrictions as to where billboards may be placed
❑ unless the billboard is put in a prominent place where the target audience is exposed to it, the advertisement will not be noticed

Although there are few small businesses that can afford to advertise on the large billboards seen next to highways and at airports, there are many who use the smaller formats next to their businesses or in the parking lots of shopping centres. Many builders and contractors make use of billboards at construction sites to advertise their services.

GUIDELINES FOR OUTDOOR ADS

❑ Identify the **product** and the **company** clearly and immediately. Use a simple background that does not compete with the message.

❑ Rely on **large illustrations** that jump out at the viewer.

❑ Use **clear, legible type**. All lowercase or a combination of uppercase and lowercase letters are best. Very bold or very thin typefaces become illegible (or unreadable) at a distance.

❑ Use **bold, brash colours**. The best colour combinations contrast in both hue and brightness. Black-on-yellow and black-on-white are two of the best combinations.

❑ Emphasize **simplicity**; short advertising copy and short words are best. Don't try to cram too much onto a billboard.

Source: Zimmerer & Scarborough, 1994:341-342.

Whatever method of advertising you choose, you should try to increase your effectiveness by following the suggestions listed below (Zimmerer & Scarborough, 1994:352):

❑ get **suppliers/manufacturers** to share the cost of the advertisement by featuring their product. A hardware store might, for instance, feature a brand of power drills in its outdoor ads and get the drill company to sponsor the board.

❑ get **other businesses** to share adverts. For example, a group of businesses in an area might take out a large advertisement in which all the businesses in the area are mentioned. This advertisement might be placed in front of a shopping centre. As another example, a calendar featuring all the businesses in a certain area might be distributed to local merchants and households.

❑ **repeat ads** that work. It saves costs and establishes a consistent image.

❑ use the same ad in **different media**. This saves the cost of having to produce a number of different advertisements.

❑ Use the services of independent **advertising specialists** and try to see if opportunities exist for exchange of services/products as payment.

❑ concentrate advertising at the **times when your target audience will listen**. Don't spread an advertisement too thinly as it will lose effect.

Where should the following businesses advertise?

❑ a furniture removal company	❑ a tavern
❑ a hairdresser	❑ a small toy manufacturer
❑ a T-shirt maker	❑ a pottery business
❑ an electrician	❑ a seamstress

11 SALES PROMOTION

Longenecker *et al*, (1994:372) gives us a useful definition of sales promotion:

> **Sales promotion is all promotional techniques that are neither personal selling nor advertising.**

Sales promotion usually complements advertising, public relations and personal selling and includes those activities designed to get customers to buy. This usually involves the cost of special offers and competitions (Frain, 1994:239).

According to Hutt & Stull (1992:270-274) there are different types of sales promotions:

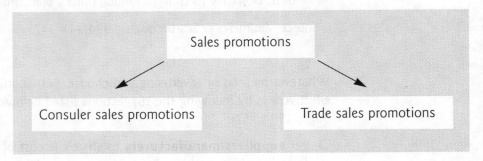

> **Consumer sales promotions are designed for and aimed at getting customers to buy.**
>
> **Trade sales promotions are aimed at getting your distribution middlemen to buy and sell large quantities of your products/services.**

11.1 Advantages and disadvantages of sales promotion

According to Marx & Van der Walt (1993:433) there are **advantages** to using sales promotion:

- ❏ it gives customers and middlemen the feeling that they are getting something extra
- ❏ it can generate quick results and is easily adaptable
- ❏ it is really useful when introducing a new product, when announcing product improvements or in support of advertising.

Serious shortcomings or **disadvantages** of sales promotion are:

- ❏ the results of this technique are short term and not lasting
- ❏ sales promotion is a support technique and should not really be used on its own

❑ care must be taken to keep everything above-board so that the sales promotion is not seen as a form of bribery

❑ sales promotions are easily copied by competitors

11.2 Sales promotion techniques

Examples of sales promotion **techniques aimed at consumers** include (Hutt & Stull, 1972:270-273):

❑ **samples**

Samples are given out free to customers or retailers to enable them to try a new product or service. For example, a butcher may braai boerewors outside the butchery to let potential customers taste his/her boerewors.

❑ **premiums**

With premiums customers get something free in or attached to a pack or by returning something to the manufacturer. For example, a real estate agency may offer free books to those customers who visit a new apartment complex selling units.

❑ **price deals**

A price deal is any short-term discount given to customers. For example, a hardware store may offer an extra 10% discount to the builders at a new construction site in the area for a period of 2 months. Remember though that price deals are easily copied, must be handled with care and should be for a short period of time only.

❑ **rebates**

In terms of rebates the customer gets some of his/her money back by filling in a form. For example, a curtain manufacturer may offer a certain cash amount back to the purchaser when he/she sends in a card included in a ready-made curtain pack.

□ **coupons**
Coupons allow customers to save money or get a free item. For example, a restaurant may offer a coupon for a free bottle of wine if the customer buys the first bottle.

□ **sponsorship of special events**
Sponsorship of special events aims to build a positive image for, or expose customers to, the business. For example, a clothing store may sponsor the local high school soccer team and gain exposure for the business.

□ **special sales**
Special sales include such popular sales as back-to-school, anniversary and clearance sales. Retailers often use this sales promotion technique.

□ **contests and games**
Contests and games are an attempt to build customer loyalty by getting customers to make repeat visits. For example, a video outlet may offer a free video contract as a prize for those customers who enter by signing their receipts from the store and putting them in a special container; the winner will be drawn

from the container at a certain date. Care needs to be taken because using contests and games in sales promotion have legal implications.

According to Hutt & Stull (1992:273-277) techniques aimed at **intermediaries and sales representatives** include:

□ **trade premium and gifts**
Trade premium and gifts involve offering gifts to dealers or sales representatives if they buy/sell more of certain products or services. For example, you might offer 3 cases of free stock to a dealer who sells 20 cases of your product. Again, care must be taken to ensure that no misunderstanding arises between the parties concerned and the promotion is not seen as a bribe.

□ **slotting allowances**
Slotting allowances are payments to a retailer for carrying an item. For example, a manufacturer of biltong may offer a one-off slotting allowance of R50.00 to all cafes that agree to stock his/her product.

❑ **advertising allowance**

An advertising allowance is a reduction in the price of the merchandise given to middlemen, in return for buying certain quantities of merchandise, to help pay for product advertising. For example, if a wholesaler agrees to a 100 case deal you might pay R250.00 for printing of pamphlets for distribution to the wholesaler's customers, promoting the particular product that the wholesaler is selling.

❑ **contests**

In terms of contests you award a prize to those who sell the most products/service. For example, the top salesperson might win a prize of a free weekend at a holiday resort.

❑ **trade shows**

Trade shows make use of display booths set up by manufacturers to display their products/services to prospective customers. The Pretoria Show often has many small business people presenting their products at booths. Specific areas of business have their own trade shows, and the small business person should find out if these are available. Examples of these shows include Decorex (interior decorating), Buildex (builders) and Computer Faire (computers and related technology)).

❑ **specialities**

Specialities are valuable articles on which the firm's name or advertising slogan appears. Examples of these are T-shirts, keyrings, pens, plaques and ashtrays. These are often used as give-aways to customers or as promotional give-aways to the trade or to middlemen.

❑ **Sales brochures**

Sales brochures allow the small business person to provide information on the company/product to dealers or customers. For example, a hiking boot manufacturer may print a brochure explaining the qualities and special features of its boots and distribute these to interested customers and potential stockists.

It is always difficult to judge the effectiveness of the sales promotion, but there are a number of areas that can help indicate **whether or not the sales promotion was successful** (Marx & Van der Walt, 1993:448):

❑ positive reactions by the sales force
❑ positive reactions by the intermediaries
❑ increases in sales patterns
❑ increase in market share
❑ positive opinion by customers
❑ high number of coupons or queries received

It is very important to keep a record of the effect of sales promotion on the business. Keep track of results before, during and after the promotion. These results need to be analysed to determine if objectives were reached and which method or combination of methods was most effective.

12 PUBLICITY

Longenecker *et al*, (1994: 374) gives a good definition of publicity:

> **Publicity is information about a business, its products or services that appears as a news item.**

Publicity is a vital part of any promotional programme for a small business, and it is important that the small business person maintain regular contact with the important people in the news media.

12.1 Advantages and disadvantages of publicity

Van der Walt *et al* (1993:449) point out a number of **advantages** of publicity:

❑ the business usually does not pay directly for publicity, although there may be some costs involved in arranging events and the like
❑ it often has high credibility in the market place because it comes from an independent source (e.g. newspaper)
❑ the news type format is more believable by customers than an advertisement and good coverage is often received.

However, publicity does have some **disadvantages**:

❑ a small businessperson has almost no control over what is published or said
❑ negative events are often used for publicity value by the news media, to the detriment of the business
❑ the small business person has little control of when the publicity appears
❑ timing may be important as in the case of a store opening

12.2 Types of publicity

A number of methods are available for getting publicity (Marx & Van der Walt, 1993:450):

❑ **a news or press release**
A news or press release is a one to two page description of a newsworthy item usually with a photograph made available to the press. For example, a bakery may send a one page description as well as a photograph, of the baking of an enormous cake to celebrate the city's birthday, to the major newspapers in the area.

☞

❏ **sponsorships**

Sponsorships were discussed earlier. For example, the bakery mentioned above may sponsor a feeding scheme for a retirement home in the area.

❏ **article**

With an article a particular aspect of news is covered in detail. For example, the bakery may provide an article to explain how a new oven saves both electricity and time.

❏ **letters**

Letters are written to the editor of a newspaper or magazine to state a point of view, give information, or disagree. For example, the bakery may write to the newspaper to compliment the city council on the help it gives the bakery in delivering its product to the retirement home.

13 PERSONAL SELLING

All businesses rely on some form of personal selling. Hutt & Stull (1992:214) provide a definition of personal selling:

> **Personal selling is one-on-one communication between the business and a customer so as to convince the customer to purchase.**

It is important to note that for personal selling to be effective the sales person must find out the needs of the customer and match the goods and services of the small business to those customer needs for the mutual benefit of both parties.

13.1 The selling process

In order to be effective the small business person needs to be able to follow the selling process in a **systematic manner** (Van der Walt *et al*, 1993:401-405).

This process includes:

❏ prospecting for customers
❏ qualifying potential customers
❏ presenting the sales message
❏ closing the sale
❏ follow-up

(a) prospecting

Prospecting is defined by Longenecker *et al* (1994:363):

Prospecting is the process of continually looking for new customers.

Prospecting means following up on leads. These leads might come from telephone directories, references and referrals, and using advertisements. Often there are computer databases available, at a price, that can generate potential customers for a product.

(b) qualify the prospects

Qualifying potential customers is important to ensure salespeople do not waste time.

Qualifying is securing prospects to find out who wants to buy and can actually buy.

The small business person can ask the following questions to see if there is the chance of a sale:

❑ Does the prospective buyer have a need for the product?
❑ Does he/she have the ability to buy?
❑ Is he/she able to make the decision to sign the deal and buy?
❑ Can you make money selling the product to him/her?

The qualifying of the potential customer may itself take a great deal of time and effort – to find out the answers to the questions mentioned above. A building contractor, for example, may have to visit a prospective customer, give a quote, discuss the requirements and adapt the offer to him/her. In this instance we can see that it would be difficult to qualify such a customer over the telephone.

(c) present the sales message

This is the **crux** of the sale. Remember that the message must be tailored to the customer. The message should have the following aspects to it:

❑ **introduce** – stimulate interest and establish contact
❑ **identify problem and need** – establish yourself as the problem solver
❑ **demonstrate product** – show the product use to the customer
❑ **handle objections** – be prepared to counter these by thinking them out beforehand

(d) close the sale
Here you reassure the customer and get agreement as to the sale.

(e) follow up
In this step you ensure the buyer is fully satisfied with the product or service and that you have met all their expectations.

| QUESTIONS SALESPEOPLE SHOULD BE ABLE TO ANSWER ||
PRODUCTS	SERVICES
How will this product meet my needs?	How will this service meet my needs?
How is it constructed?	What are the advantages and disadvantages of buying this service?
How do I take care of this product?	What are the risks if I buy this service?
What is the warranty?	What is the scope and duration of the service?
How do I use this product?	How do I use this service?
How does it work?	How does it work?
How much does this product cost and is it economical?	How much does this service cost and is it economical?
How does this product compare to those offered by the competition?	How does this service compare to those offered by the competition?
What is the reputation of the manufacturer?	What is the reputation the supplier?
What services usually accompany this product?	What products usually accompany this service?

Source: Adapted from Hutt, R.W. & Stull, W.A. 1992. *Marketing: an introduction*. South Western: Cincinnati, p. 115.

It is especially important to be able to translate features of a product or service into the benefits that it gives the customer – because customers buy benefits, not products or features. For example, if a person buys a telephone answering machine with one-touch control and a warranty as features, the benefits he/she is looking for are ease of operation and peace of mind. Note that the salesperson needs to make sure he/she realises exactly what customer he/she is selling to, so as to be able to tie in to the benefits that are important to that customer.

14 SUMMARY

The use of marketing communication techniques by a small business requires the business person to think creatively and innovatively. This is because the communication campaign will require the use of scarce business resources. Thus the planning and controlling of communication efforts will be of the utmost importance. As a small business person you must be able to identify what is successful and what is not, and to ensure that all resources that are used help to achieve the overall goals of the business.

15 SELF-EVALUATION

15.1 Terms you have learned

Explain each of the following terms:

- ❑ promotion
- ❑ promotion mix
- ❑ target audience
- ❑ advertising
- ❑ sales promotion
- ❑ consumer sales promotions
- ❑ publicity
- ❑ message content
- ❑ message form
- ❑ promotion budget
- ❑ personal advertising
- ❑ institutional advertising
- ❑ trade sales promotions
- ❑ personal selling

15.2 Quiz

(i) What four factors must be considered in determining a promotion mix?

1. .... 2. ....

3. .... 4. ....

(ii) List three possible objectives of promotion

1. ....

2. ....

3. ....

(iii) What is the difference between message content and message form? Explain.

....

....

....

....

(iv) List five ways of setting the promotional budget?

1. .... 2. ....

3. .... 4. ....

5. ....

(v) What are the different types of advertising?

1.	2.

(vi) List the advantages/disadvantages of the following media types:

MEDIA	ADVANTAGE	DISADVANTAGE
❏ Newspaper ❏ Radio ❏ Magazine ❏ Outdoor		

(vi) Explain how it is possible to increase the effectiveness of advertising.

....

....

....

....

(viii) List five types of sales promotion techniques aimed at consumers.

1. ....

2. ....

3. ....

4. ....

5. ....

(ix) What are four methods of checking whether a promotion was successful?

1.	2.
3.	4.

(x) How can small business people get publicity for their small businesses?

1. ....

2. ....

3. ....

4. ....

(xi) What four questions can help in qualifying a prospective customer?

1. ....

2. ....

3. ....

4. ....

(xii) Fill in the 7 steps in communicating with customers

15.3 Case Study

EASY WAVES: THE LOOK OF TODAY

Easy Waves used a number of marketing communication techniques to communicate with its customers. These are discussed below.

Sales promotion

A promotions company specialising in township store promotions was employed. This strategy involved using demonstrators to educate consumers about hair care and to promote the Easy Waves range. As inducements for trial, trial size sachets of the range and price-off coupons on the main products were also utilised.

Advertising

The development of an advertising campaign was based, from the very early stages, on a strong and distinctive identity for Easy Waves. Even though the initial media budget was limited, an attempt was made to develop a powerful creative advertisement which would stand out from that of the competition, would be distinctive and different, and would generate immediate interest. The majority of Easy Waves's competitors were focusing on very straightforward advertisements, primarily utilising an approach showing models with "successful" hair. The Easy Waves campaign was to establish a pay-off for the brand with respect to image.

The result of this was what was considered to be a sophisticated family advertisement in a social setting (totally different to any competitor's advertisements). Each Easy Waves advertisement ended with the same pay-off line of "Feeling Soft, Looking Good!" Even in the early stages of introduction there was positive reaction from the trade and consumers to the advertisement – particularly to the pay-off line.

Initially only print advertising in the black media was used. Print was used because it is a credible medium: it enables the advertiser to be descriptive as well as having a long life for the advertisement. An important decision during the latter part of the introductory phase was to extend the advertising campaign into radio, utilising music, which is a powerful communication vehicle in the black market.

THE REASONS FOR UTILISING RADIO ADVERTISING

❑ Radio has very good penetration in the black consumer market particularly in the outer urban and rural areas. This was an important factor as Easy Waves had identified a golden opportunity in these areas where competition was less established. This allowed Easy Waves to gain an advantage in these areas at a relatively low cost as competitive advertising was minimal. For example, Easy Waves began advertising in the Lesotho area for roughly R1 000 per month, realising substantial monthly sales in a very short time.

❑ Magazine penetration in the outer urban and rural areas was not good and readership levels were low, while radio had a strong presence.

❑ Radio can be easily utilised as a frequent reminder medium, which is important for any new product. It is also an urgent medium and overcomes the literacy problem of many consumers.

❑ Television advertising has limited penetration particularly in rural areas and is therefore less effective than radio.

Source: Van der Walt, A. & Machado, R. (eds.). 1992. *New marketing success stories.* Southern: Johannesburg, pp. 87-88.

(i) What type of sales promotion did Easy Waves use?

(ii) What illustration did Easy Waves use in its consumer advertisement? Why?

(iii) Why was radio used to advertise Easy Waves?

(iv) When the company first started advertising what media did it used and why?

16 REFERENCES

Adcock, D., Bradfield, R., Halborg, A. & Ross, C. 1993. *Marketing principles and practice*. Pitman: London.

Anderson, A.H. & Dobson, T. 1994. *Effective marketing*. Blackwell: Oxford.

Ennew, C.T. 1993. *The marketing blueprint*. Blackwell: Oxford.

Frain, J. 1994. *Introduction to marketing*. Pitman: London.

Giles, G.B. 1994. *Marketing*. Pitman: London.

Hutt, R.W. & Stull, W.A. 1992. *Marketing: an introduction*. South Western: Cincinnati.

Longenecker, J.G., Moore, C.W. & Petty, J.W. 1994. *Small business management: an entrepreneurial emphasis*. South Western: Cincinnati.

Marx, S. & Van der Walt, A.(eds.). 1992. *Marketing management*. Juta: Cape Town.

Van der Walt, A. & Machado, R.(eds.). 1992. *New marketing success stories*. Southern: Johannesburg.

Zimmerer, T.W. & Scarborough, N.M. 1994. *Essentials of small business management*. Macmillan: New York.

THE MARKETING PLAN: PUTTING IT ALL TOGETHER

8

1 LEARNING OBJECTIVES

After you have studied this chapter you should be able to:

- ❑ explain what is meant by marketing planning
- ❑ identify why a marketing plan is useful
- ❑ make marketing planning more effective
- ❑ discuss the various components of a marketing plan
- ❑ evaluate the current marketing situation of a small business
- ❑ give a definition of a marketing strategy

2 INTRODUCTION

Any business, small or large, needs to decide how to proceed with marketing the business. This aspect of running a business is called the marketing planning process and is defined by McDonald (1992:3).

> **The marketing planning process is deciding on a logical sequence of activities, leading to the setting of marketing objectives and the plans for achieving them.**

Marketing planning is the game plan which the small business needs if it hopes to achieve success in the market place. The result of the marketing planning process is the marketing plan.

> **The marketing plan is the result of the marketing planning process and sets out what the business wants to achieve through its marketing, how it will achieve this and how much investment this will take.**

By setting down what the business aims to achieve (your business goals and objectives) and thinking critically about your business you can achieve the principal purpose of marketing planning, which is identifying and creating your competitive edge (McDonald, 1992:3).

Since the environment in which the small business operates is becoming ever more complex, dynamic and competitive, a business without a good marketing plan will have little chance of success.

Helping you to identify and create your competitive edge, and helping you cope with the environment are but two of the benefits that marketing planning provides.

A marketing plan is also useful for the following reasons (McDonald & Tideman, 1993:14):

❏ it forces you as a business person to follow an organised approach
❏ it helps establish specific directions for your business
❏ it helps the business to be consistent in its actions
❏ it sets objectives and direction for the business

There are certain strategies that you can follow to ensure that your marketing planning is effective. These include the following (McDonald & Tideman, 1993:6-9):

❏ **try to establish where you want your business to be in two to three years time** – then decide what you need to do within the next year in order to get there. It is important to plan this way rather than simply planning for one year at a time so that you know where your actions and efforts are leading.

❏ **always organise marketing activities around customer groups.** This will focus attention on the most important aspect of any business – your customers.

❏ **make sure you gather as much specific information about the business environment as possible.** A marketing plan is only as good as the information about the environment, customers, competitors and markets upon which it is based.

❏ **keep the plan and the process simple.** You want effective action, not "paralysis by analysis" or mountains of information through which to wade. Try to focus on the key aspects of your business and its environment.

❏ **if you are unsure of what you are doing, take steps to get the necessary skills and knowledge.** There are many good basic business and marketing books and courses geared towards small business people.

3 WRITE THE MARKETING PLAN

It is important that you write down your marketing plan and document your decisions. **The question is: What process do you follow?** Most marketing plans will contain similar steps and be fairly close to the sequence shown below. The process begins with analysis of the current situation and ends with how you will ensure you achieve your objectives (Gerson, 1991:10).

> **FIGURE 8.1**
> **COMPONENTS OF THE MARKETING PLAN**
>
> 1. Executive summary
> 2. Current marketing situation
> 3. Marketing analysis
> 4. Set objectives
> 5. Decide on marketing strategy
> 6. Draw up action programmes
> 7. Projected profit/loss statement and budget
> 8. Establish controls
>
> Source: Adapted from Kotler, P. & Armstrong, G. 1991. *Principles of marketing.* 5th edition. Prentice-Hall: Englewood Cliffs, p. 539.

We will discuss each of these components and relate them to the previous chapters.

8.1 EXECUTIVE SUMMARY

The executive summary is simply a summary of the **main goals, decisions and recommendations** that are in the actual marketing plan (Kotler & Armstrong, 1991:539-541). Generally, the executive summary briefly describes your marketing plans, the product or service you offer, your target markets, who your competitors are and the level of sales you expect to achieve.

The executive summary is especially important if you are presenting your plan to a **banker or funding agency**. It gives a concise summary of your plan (Gerson, 1991:12) without prospective funders having to read the detailed plan.

Note that the executive summary is written **after** the marketing plan is written.

8.2 CURRENT MARKETING SITUATION

This section of the marketing plan describes the current situation with regard to the marketing activities of the small business. This section applies both to an established business or a new business. It includes information on the following areas:

❑ **market description**
The market description identifies the major market segments and target markets. This includes customer profiles and the factors that influence customers and their purchases.

❑ **product review**

The product review shows the sales, prices and profit margins of the major products in the product mix.

❑ **competitive review**

The competitive review identifies your major competitors and their marketing mixes.

❑ **distribution review**

The distribution review identifies developments in the distribution channels of the business. This includes any changes in the channels and the motivations of the middlemen.

❑ **broad business environment analysis**

The broad business environment analysis analyses the trends in the broad business environment that might affect the business or its customers. Areas of importance are the economy, legislation, socio-cultural changes or technological developments.

The important thing with this current marketing situation analysis is to be specific as to the effect of the economy of your business or customers. For example, saying "the economy is bad" is vague and unclear – it would be clearer to say that a more competitive economy is leading your customers to look for high quality, lower-priced products.

EXAMPLES OF SOME VARIABLES IN THE BROAD BUSINESS ENVIRONMENT		
ECONOMIC	**LEGISLATION**	**SOCIO-CULTURAL**
❑ inflation	❑ union legislation	❑ demographic changes
❑ interest rates	❑ privatisation	❑ lifestyle changes
❑ tax levels	❑ environmental laws	❑ housing changes
❑ VAT rates	❑ regional policies	❑ education levels
❑ minimum wages	❑ local council laws	❑ urbanisation
❑ import tariffs	❑ RDP programmes	❑ disposable income levels

Source: Adapted from McDonald, M.H.B. & Tideman, C.C.S. 1993. *Retail marketing plans: how to prepare them, how to use them.* Butterworth-Heinemann: Oxford, p. 23.

3.3 Marketing analysis

The marketing analysis requires you to make some judgements about your business. It is important that you do not rush through this component, as your success in business will, to a large extent, depend on how well you know your own business.

The basic objective of this activity is to organise the major findings regarding your marketing situation and your knowledge of your own business relative to competitors. One way of doing this is to use a SWOT analysis (McDonald & Tideman, 1993:27).

A SWOT analysis is a summary of the major findings of your current situation analysis under the headings of strengths (S), weaknesses (W), opportunities (O) and threats (T).

It is important to know exactly what these terms mean and Gerson (1991:16) provides us with definitions.

Strengths are things you do well and that set you apart from competitors.

Weaknesses are areas on which you need to improve, if you do not want your competitors to get an advantage.

Opportunities are those things that can benefit your business.

Threats are those things that can hurt your business.

It is important to focus on key factors only, and highlight your business's strengths/weaknesses relative to both competitors and the opportunities and threats that exist in the environment.

Strengths and weaknesses are identified by looking at your business relative to competitors. Examples of strengths might be a strong brand, good relations with distributors or a good sales force. Possible weaknesses might be a lack of financing, a poor location or a lack of promotional activities.

FIGURE 8.2
SWOT ANALYSIS

STRENGTHS	WEAKNESSES
OPPORTUNITIES	THREATS

Examples of potential opportunities include competitor's businesses that close, increased customer activity or special promotions. Examples of possible threats might be new competitors entering your area, price increases from your suppliers or possible strikes by employees. Try to find areas in which your competitors are weak and in which you can capitalise on your strengths.

It should be clear that your customer profile and competitor analysis can help you determine what your SWOT analysis will look like.

3.4 Set objectives

The next step in the process is to set marketing objectives (McDonald, 1991:47).

A marketing objective is what you want to achieve through your marketing during the time frame of the plan.

Marketing objectives are about **products, customers** and **markets.** Most marketing plans, however, usually **include both financial and marketing objectives.** Note that financial objectives can only be reached by achieving marketing objectives.

For example, a bakery may have the following financial objectives:

❑ net profits of R100 000 for 1995
❑ cash flow of R200 000 for 1995
❑ a return on investment of 20% for 1995

The bakery's marketing objectives may be:

❑ 30% increase in sales for 1995
❑ customer awareness of the bakery increased from 30% to 60% in 1995
❑ ten new distributors for its products in the first 6 months of the year

Note the general form of the objectives:

❑ **they are quantifiable**
Try to express objectives in terms of numbers or values. Also try to state the level at which you are starting and the level you wish to achieve. Avoid general terms such as "maximise" and "increase".

❑ **they are ranked in order of importance**
This helps you to focus on the most important issues.

☞

> ❏ **they specify a time**
> Mention by when you want to achieve each objective.
>
> ❏ **they are reasonable**
> Objectives should be a challenge but they should be realistic and attainable. Do not overstate your objectives – ensure that you believe that it is definitely possible to achieve your goals.

8.5 Decide on your marketing strategy

McDonald (1993:47) gives a useful definition of a strategy.

> **A strategy is how you plan to achieve your objectives.**

A marketing strategy requires you to decide on your **target market,** your **positioning** and your **marketing mix** in order to satisfy your target markets.

The process of choosing a target market is explained in Chapter 3, while positioning a product and the marketing mix are explained in chapters 4 – 7.

A brief summary of the various **aspects of the marketing mix** as applied to the bakery example we have mentioned before, include:

❏ **target market** – housewives in the area, cafes, restaurants and retail outlets in the city

❏ **positioning** – good-tasting, homemade, healthy bakery goods

❏ **product line** – breads, confectionery, special cakes and hamburger buns

❏ **price** – no more than 10% above major competitors on cakes and confectionery goods and parity with major competitors on breads and buns.

❏ **distribution** – concentrated on retail outlets and aiming to increase stores stocking products by 25% in 6 months. Also concentrating on restaurants.

❏ **Marketing communication** – personal call on restaurants, special deals for new stockists, competitions for volume customers, birthday promotions aimed at mothers in local area, and so on.

Note that this is only a summary of the major decisions on each of the marketing mix areas. As was shown in chapters 4 – 7, the process of deciding on what to do with each area can be quite detailed and requires much information.

3.6 Draw up action programmes

The marketing strategy, as we stated earlier, tells you how the marketing objectives are going to be achieved. The action plan is the specific programme of action to implement the strategies. The action programme **shows when activities will be started, reviewed and completed.** As Kotler & Armstrong (1991:542) point out, it answers the following questions:

❏ exactly **what** will be done?
❏ **when** will it be done?
❏ **who** will do it?
❏ **how much** will it cost?

The action programme assigns activities to specific people to get things done by a certain time. If a small business does not have many personnel resources careful attention needs to be given to the timing of the activities so that a realistic time estimate can be made. This is especially true for a one-person business.

3.7 Projected profit/loss statement and budget

By doing a detailed action programme you will be able to develop a profit and loss statement for the business that **reflects the projected effect of the marketing plan on the business.**

There are many personal computer programmes that make it easier than the traditional manual methods to generate a profit and loss statement. The process of setting budgets was discussed in chapter 7; setting budgets focuses the efforts of the small business on achieving its objectives. Setting budgets also helps in deciding on the numerous requests for advertising/promotion made on many small business owners. "Does it fit in with my marketing plan?" and "Is it within my budget?" should be the criteria against which you evaluate all these options.

3.8 Set up controls

Implementing the marketing plan cannot take into account all the possible surprises that might occur. This means that the small business must **ensure that the planned results are achieved.** This is done through marketing control (Kotler & Armstrong, 1991:555).

Marketing control is the measuring and evaluating of the results of the marketing plan and taking the necessary corrective actions for success.

Areas of importance here are **sales analysis, profitability, expenses-to-sales ratios** and **customer research.**

It is also important to regularly **monitor performance** in terms of the marketing objectives, because if you wait too long it will be too late to do anything to correct problems. One helpful technique is to try to think of possible **contingency plans** for unexpected events. This will help you to think of potential pitfalls and increase your ability to react speedily to possible surprises.

4 SELF-EVALUATION

4.1 Terms you have learned

Explain each of the following terms:

- ❑ marketing planning process
- ❑ marketing plan
- ❑ executive summary
- ❑ SWOT analysis
- ❑ marketing objective
- ❑ marketing strategy

- ❑ strength
- ❑ weakness
- ❑ opportunity
- ❑ threat
- ❑ strategy
- ❑ marketing control

4.2 Quiz

Answer the following questions

(i) What is the principal purpose of marketing planning?

....

....

(ii) List six benefits that a marketing plan provides for a small business:

1. .... 2. ....

3. .... 4. ....

5. .... 6. ....

(iii) How can you ensure your marketing planning is effective?

1. ....

2. ....

3. ....

4. ....

5. ....

(iv) Identify the eight components of a marketing plan.

1. ....

2. ....

3. ....

4. ....

5. ....

6. ....

7. ....

8. ....

(v) In what circumstances would the executive summary be especially important?

....

....

(vi) In what five areas is information needed for an analysis of the current marketing situation?

1. ....   2. ....

3. ....   4. ....

5. ....

(vii) Briefly describe the four components of a SWOT analysis and discuss how the four components influence your marketing plan.

1.	2.
3.	4.

(viii)   What is the difference between financial and marketing objectives?

....

....

(ix)   Name four characteristics of good marketing objectives.

1. ....

2. ....

3. ....

4. ....

5. ....

(x)   What three aspects make up a marketing strategy?

1. ....

2. ....

3. ....

(xi)   List four questions which a good action plan answers.

Question 1: ....

2: ....

3: ....

4: ....

4.3   Case Study

EASY WAVES: SITUATION ANALYSIS

The following marketing environment effects were identified at the launch of Easy Waves.

Along with the rapid urbanisation of the black population was the fact that the demographic profile of the white population is ageing while the black population has a younger profile. This is important as the cosmetic/hair care market is aimed at the younger sectors of the market. This, tied to the growing disposable income and spending power of the black consumer, positively influenced the entry of Easy Waves into the market.

Together with the growing affluence of the black consumer was a growing trend towards sophistication and a rise in the aspirations of the black consumer. This trend was most vividly illustrated by the new and individual "Afro" hair styles, and more particularly the wet-look perm. It is not surprising to note that these styles were inspired by black American hairstyles. Black Americans serve as role models and are an important reference group for the emerging black urban consumer in South Africa. In fact, a number of black consumers insist on using very expensive imported American hair care products.

THE INDICATORS OF GOLDEN OPPORTUNITY FOR EASY WAVES

❑ a rapidly growing market
❑ several, but not firmly established, competitors
❑ no major established company present in the market place
❑ a lack of sophisticated marketing techniques being employed in the market place. Rudimentary packaging and promotion
❑ very low advertising-to-sales ratios in the industry
❑ inadequate distribution levels, especially through outlets

In spite of these favourable trends, however, the situation was different a few years later.

Developments in the black hair care market highlight the difficulties faced by marketers such as Easy Waves in dealing with this sector. The general feeling was that the black hair care market was changing, and that the booming growth of 1985/86 had not stabilised and was slowing down. There were a number of other problems facing marketers.

One serious problem was the proliferation of products offered by both multi-national companies and home-market operators resulting in confusion for both the trade and consumer. There were an estimated 100 companies fighting for a piece of the black hair care market, conservatively estimated at more than R200 million a year. The large number of competitors led to a credibility problem, with some products not living up to the claims made for them.

Another problem was the fight among outlets (retailers, cash-and-carry whole-salers and hair salons) for a share of the market. Some salons were successfully retailing gels, sprays and so on in direct competition with the chain stores. The salons, which often carry the exclusive professional lines, were able to exert influence on the consumers to buy a specific brand as that used for the perm. Retail chains countered with home-perm type products and lower prices to draw customers away from the salons.

Another result of the proliferation of brands was the choice presented to con-sumers, as well as the possibility of buying a line that dies quickly or rejecting one that subsequently booms in popularity! It has been noted that brand loy-alty is almost non-existent in the black hair care market and that market shares are unsure and subject to fluctuation.

Despite all these problems there was evidence of increased sales through the retail outlets and that supermarkets were beginning to settle on the better sup-ported brands.

Adapted from Van der Walt, A. & Machado, R. (eds.). 1992. *New marketing success stories.* Southern: Johannesburg, pp. 83-90.

1. Identify the major environmental trends affecting the marketing of Easy Waves.
2. List the analysis areas at which Easy Waves looked (e.g. competition, distribution, etc.).
3. What were the critical developments for Easy Waves in the market place in terms of a SWOT analysis?

REFERENCES

Gerson, R.F. 1991. *Writing and implementing a marketing plan.* Crisp Publications: Los Altos.

Kotler, P. & Armstrong, G. 1991. *Principles of marketing.* 5th edition. Prentice-Hall: Englewood Cliffs.

McDonald, M.H.B. 1992. *The marketing planner.* Butterworth-Heineman: Oxford.

McDonald, M.H.B & Tideman, C.C.S. 1993. *Retail marketing plans: how to prepare them, how to use them.* Butterworth-Heinemann: Oxford.

Van der Walt, A. & Machado, R. (eds). 1992. *New marketing success stories.* Southern: Johannesburg.